D1348330

ARCHAEOLOGICAL SITES OF THE LAKE DISTRICT

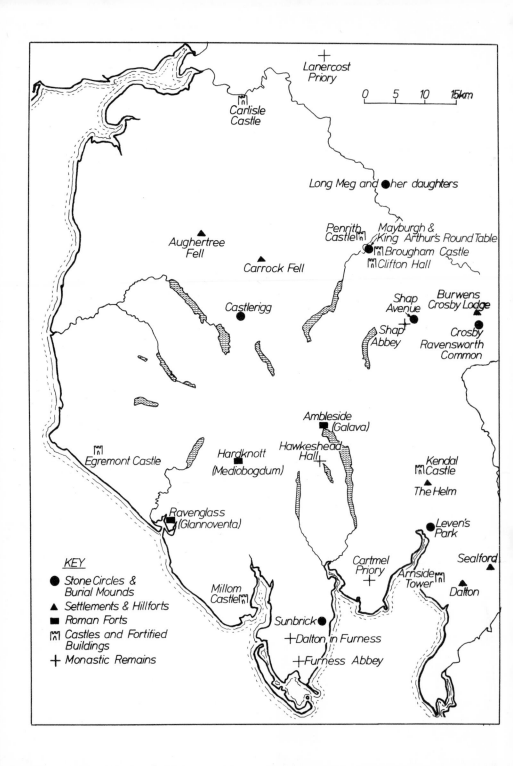

Lanercost
Priory

Carlisle
Castle

0 5 10 15km

Long Meg and her daughters

Aughertree
Fell

Penrith
Castle

Mayburgh &
King Arthur's Round Table
Brougham Castle
Clifton Hall

Carrock Fell

Castlerigg

Shap
Avenue

Burwens
Crosby Lodge

Shap
Abbey

Crosby
Ravensworth
Common

Ambleside
(Galava)

Hawkeshead
Hall

Egremont Castle

Hardknott
(Mediobogdum)

Kendal
Castle

The Helm

Ravenglass
(Glannoventa)

Leven's
Park

KEY

Stone Circles &
Burial Mounds

Settlements & Hillforts

Roman Forts

Castles and Fortified
Buildings

Monastic Remains

Cartmel
Priory

Sealford

Arnside
Tower

Dalton

Millom
Castle

Sunbrick

Dalton in Furness

Furness Abbey

ARCHAEOLOGICAL SITES
OF THE
LAKE DISTRICT

T Clare

MOORLAND PUBLISHING CO.

British Library Cataloguing in Publication Data

Clare, T.
  Archaeological sites of the Lake District.
  1. Historic sites — Lake District (Cumbria)
  2. Lake District (Cumbria) — Antiquities
  I. Title
  942.7'8'012   DA670.L1

  ISBN 0-86190-015-4 (Hardback)
  ISBN 0-86190-014-6 (Paperback)

Printed in Great Britain by
Butler & Tanner Ltd, Frome
Moorland Publishing Co Ltd,
PO Box 2, 9-11 Station Street,
Ashbourne, Derbyshire,
DE6 1DZ.

Contents

Introduction: Continuity and
Evolution of the Landscape / 7
**Stone Circles and Burial
Mounds / 9**
1   Long Meg and her daughters / 9
2   Mayburgh and King Arthur's Round
Table / 11
3   Castlerigg, Keswick / 13
4   Shap Avenue / 15
5   Crosby Ravensworth Common / 16
6   Leven's Park Ringcairn / 18
7   Sunbrick Stone Circle / 20
Settlements and Hillforts / 21
8   Aughertree Fell / 23
9   Carrock Fell / 25
10   Burwens, Crosby lodge / 27
11   The Helm / 29
12   Sealford / 30
13   Dalton / 32
Roman Forts / 34
14   Ambleside / 35

15   Hardknott / 39
16   Walls Castle, Ravenglass / 46
**Castles and Fortified
Buildings / 48**
17   Carlisle Castle and City Walls / 50
18   Penrith / 58
19   Brougham / 64
20   Clifton Hall / 76
21   Egremont / 78
22   Kendal / 82
23   Millom / 86
24   Arnside Tower / 92
Monastic Remains / 96
25   Lanercost Priory / 97
26   Shap Abbey / 108
27   Hawkeshead Hall / 120
28   Cartmel Priory / 122
29   Dalton in Furness / 128
30   Furness Abbey / 129
Glossary / 154
Index / 156

Preface

This is a guide to both individual sites and the principal types of monuments. The geographical position of the sites is shown on the following map but in the text they are grouped by type. Each site is described separately but a comparison of similar examples is also made. The description of the type in general may be used irrespective of which site (or sites) has been visited.

The chosen sites are good examples of their type and either have public access or are adjacent to public rights of way. In the latter cases — Burwens, Sealford and Dalton — it would be courteous to seek permission from the farmer first. All sites are Ancient Monuments and as such it is an offence to deface, damage or disturb them or their environs. Equally the Country Code should be followed.

Each site has a ground plan marked with several viewpoints. These refer to the corresponding illustrations and show the features of special interest that may be seen from that spot, and their significance is explained in the accompanying notes.

Acknowledgements

The writer wishes to thank the vicars of Lanercost and Cartmel for allowing their churches to be included and Mr Mason-Hornby, Carlisle City Council, The British Museum and The Royal Aircraft Establishment, Farnborough, for permission to reproduce or make use of, respectively, the estate plan of Dalton Village, the initial letter of Edward II's Charter to Carlisle, the self portrait of a Furness monk and a Landsat photo of Cumbria. Nor should those who read and commented upon the draft manuscript and, in particular J. Hughes FSA, be forgotten.

The plans and drawings reproduced in this book are based on the following:
Page 2: Landsat 220/022/28/5/1977; pages 10 and 13: CW(1), **V**, 39ff; page 25: CW(2), **XXXVIII**, 37; page 38: CW(2), **XVI**, 57; page 39: CW(2), **XXVIII**, 314; page 51: Nutter, *Carlisle in Olden Times*; page 52: Curwen, 1913, 108; page 58: CW(2), **XXX**, 12; page 64: RCHM, 1936, 58; page 82: Curwen, 1913, 146; page 86: CW(2), **XXIV**, 180; page 92: RCHM, 1936, 14; page 121: Beck, 1844, *Annales Furnesiensis*; page 122: CW(2), **XLV**, 49; page 129: CW(2), **LXVII**, 61.

Abbreviations
CW(1): *Transactions of the Cumberland and Westmorland Antiquarian Society (Old Series)*
CW(2): *Transactions of the Cumberland and Westmorland Antiquarian Society (New Series)*
RCHM, 1936: Royal Commission Historical Monuments (Westmorland)
Curwen, 1913: *The Castles and Fortified Towers of Cumberland, Westmorland and Lancashire, North of the Sands* (Kendal, 1913)

Introduction: Continuity and the Evolution of the Landscape

The first farming, characteristic of the Neolithic, was introduced to the Lake District no later than in Southern England. The principal surviving monuments are, however, late in the period and are related to those of the Early Bronze Age showing there was continuity instead of the change implied by the separate terms of 'Neolithic' and 'Bronze Age'. The principal sites of that date are circular burial mounds, stone circles and unenclosed huts. Sites belonging to the Late Bronze Age cannot be identified with certainty but by analogy with elsewhere they could consist of hillforts and settlements of the type still in use or refurbished in the post-Roman period.

The Romans identified the population with the much larger tribal grouping known as the Brigantes. During that period small towns grew up around forts such as Brougham, Ambleside and at Carlisle where the settlement continued to expand after the fort had been moved. That no town grew up around Hardknott shows factors other than the presence of forts were necessary to generate town growth. It seems likely that most Roman forts, but not Hardknott, were at existing focal or market points albeit these functional centres had never become built up. Only Carlisle was big enough to resist the post-Roman trend of urban decay. It, together with the Lyvennet, may have become the centres of Urien's kingdom of Rheged

which collapsed with his murder sometime during 570-590. Within a generation or so the area had been partitioned, the northern part being absorbed by the kingdom in South West Scotland, the later Strathclyde, with perhaps, a separate principality in the Copeland/Ravenglass area.

As these political arrangements survived until William II conquered the area in 1092 it is hardly surprising to find them reflected in the Norman land divisions. Thus the cairn on Dunmail Raise marked both the boundary of Cumberland and of Strathclyde. Tradition and pollen analysis both suggest this boundary was fixed in the 10th century: tradition relates that the cairn covers king Dunmail who reigned in that century and pollen shows that the valley to the north was first cleared about that time.

Until the 16th century two important factors in the local economy and landscape were the impact of the monasteries, either by direct farming or land ownership, and the Scottish raids. The latter combined with the Black Death produced economic decline. A smaller population must also have allowed agriculture to retreat from the more marginal land. Presumably the population had regained its former size by the early 19th century when rural depopulation again occurred with the drift to industrial towns. This trend has to some extent been counterbalanced by 'commuting'

Dunmail Raise

and second home ownership.

While, therefore, the individual forts, castles and abbeys which have survived are interesting and important in themselves they are only parts of landscapes which previously existed. The prehistoric and Roman sites which have survived to the present time would also be part of the medieval landscape and require explanation, hence the stories of Walls Castle, Long Meg and the Round Table. At any one time, therefore, the landscape was and is the product of current land use and what has been inherited. The Beaker burials at Levens made use of an old area of settlement, the Romano-British farmer at Burwens used or modified the field system he found while at Shap the present limit of intensive farming is very similar to the monastic boundaries. Many fields today are three, four or more centuries old and although the Elizabethan farmhouse that went with them is protected, they are not. At Shap the limit of intensive land use has been static or advanced slightly, but at Aughertree farming has fallen back.

Many sites — Aughertree, Crosby Ravensworth, Levens and Burwens — are in areas which have not been cultivated in more than five hundred years so that the distribution of archaeological sites is a distribution of past and present land use. Stray finds and aerial photography show there were many Burwens in the lowlands and the evidence suggests that some lie beneath present villages.

The detection and recording of this mass of lost information is a formidable, perhaps insuperable task; so it is fortunate that some sites have survived on the fringes of present farmland. There are, however, two problems. First, are these surviving sites safe, will an expansion of farming, afforestation or mineral works not destroy them? Secondly, are they representative of the lost sites of the lowlands? If transhumance (the seasonal movement of animals) was practised then some of the well preserved upland settlements must have been summer steadings. This would explain why some do not have fields, because the latter were elsewhere. Clearly there is much to do before we understand the archaeological sites of the Lake District and their relationship to past and present landscapes.

Stone Circles and Burial Mounds

The Origins of Stone Circles

Most circular ritual sites date to the Neolithic-Early Bronze Age. Four principal types may be recognised: simple burial mounds, stone circles, ring cairns and henges. Stone circles come in many forms. They can be freestanding (eg Long Meg), kerbs around cairns (Crosby Ravensworth **2D**), or be beneath mounds (Crosby Ravensworth **4**). In ring cairns, (eg Levens) earthen or stone banks performed much the same function. In the henge monument (eg Mayburgh) bank and stone circle come together.

Stone circles, ring cairns and henges all involved the definition of a circular area within which burials were sometimes made — Sunbrick, Levens, the Round Table, Gaythorne Plain **3** and **4** and perhaps Aughertree Fell (for the latter see p 23). Carvings at Long Meg also recall burial practices. At Sunbrick, Levens and Gaythorne **3** and **4** the circular area was sealed by a mound or pavement. Astronomical alignments are claimed only for the freestanding stone circles, probably because they have not been sought in the other types. A notable feature is the rarity of an alignment on the midsummer sun and the low height of the stones at Keswick and Sunbrick must have made observation of celestial bodies above them difficult. Astronomy does not account for the bank surrounding the stones at Mayburgh, the circular form of the sites or features such as the entrance and rectangle of Keswick and the 'porch' of Long Meg. These features are, however, paralleled in the henges and ring cairns.

The ring cairn at Levens could not be distinguished from the remains of a hut and it is interesting, therefore, that a number of stone circles and henges elsewhere replaced or contained in their first phase timber buildings or huts. Contemporary with such timber buildings was a tradition of building special huts for the dead (mortuary huts).

The development of stone circles and ring cairns from such huts or buildings would account for all the observed features. The big circles continued the tradition of the great buildings, the small circles echoed the mortuary huts. The presence of astronomical alignments and burials in some of the large sites may have been incidental to the use to which such places were put, just as many churches are orientated to the east and have burials in and around them without either being their primary function. There are, however specialist churches (shrines and cemetery chapels) just as there are circles with wholly funerary associations. As places of gathering the big circles were located at focal points — the crossing of the Eamont (Mayburgh) or the meeting of three valleys (Keswick).

1 LONG MEG AND HER DAUGHTERS
NY 57103722

The site comprises an outlier of red sandstone ▶ **A**, Long Meg, and a 'circle' of geologically different boulders **B**, her daughters. As the name implies there is a tradition that the stones are petrified people. In places they appear to be set in a low bank but this is probably no more than a 'headland' at the end of a ploughed area.

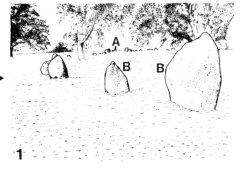

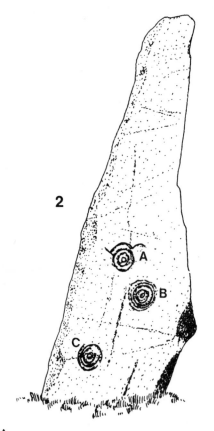

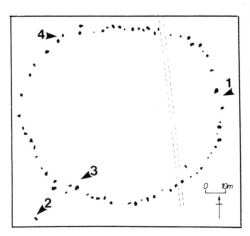

2

▲
The side of Long Meg facing the circle is decorated both with modern initials and three prehistoric designs — cup and ring **A**, a spiral **B** and concentric circles **C** — usually found in sites with a predominantly funerary purpose dating from the Middle Neolithic to Early Bronze Age. It is impossible to say whether these early carvings were added before or after the stone's erection or even whether they are directly connected with the circle. Viewed from the hypothetical centre of the circle, however, Long Meg is in exactly the right position for the midwinter sun to set over it.

The circumference near to Long Meg turns outwards like a porch, its two sides **A** and **B** being formed of two stones each. Oddly, Long Meg **C** is not on the centre line of this 'porch' but to one side. The reason cannot be guessed at but if the circle and outlier was primarily an astronomical device aligned on the midwinter sun should the 'porch' not have been also? Indeed, the stones at **B** would seem to have hidden the lower part of Long Meg from anyone at the centre of the circle.
▼

3

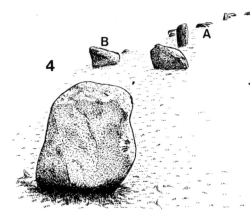

4

B

A

◄At **A** the circumference is much flatter than elsewhere, almost a straight line. It is, however, difficult without excavation, to be quite sure whether stones such as **B** have fallen over or are in their original position. There is an 18th century story that the farmer started to remove the stones but, after a night with the worst thunderstorm Cumberland had known, put them back. It is tempting to see some of the misplaced stones as his handiwork.

Little can be said of the purpose of the site but it possesses a porch-like arrangement which does not easily fit its astronomical alignment. The latter suggests stone circle builders hereabouts were not too bothered about the midsummer sun.

The 'porch' and the use of a different kind of rock for the outlier does, however, suggest order if not design and the carvings link with funerary sites.

2 MAYBURGH AND KING ARTHUR'S ROUND TABLE
NY 51922845 & 52322840

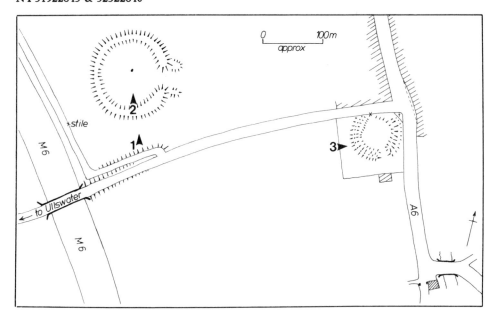

Mayburgh consists of a bank through which ▶ there is a single passageway **A**. This entrance was emphasised by an increase in the height of the bank on either side and by four standing stones in the passageway. A further feature first recorded in the 18th century is the low projection on either side of the entrance **B** which makes the plan of the monument look like a hut with a porch.

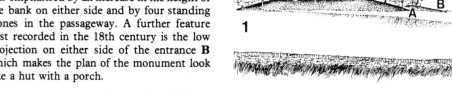

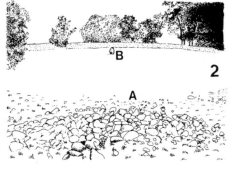

◀ Early accounts refer to a circle of standing stones at the foot of the bank **A** with four more forming a 'square' or a 'circle' in the centre. Of the latter only one now remains **B**. The construction of the bank from thousands of stones rather than upcast from a ditch must have been deliberate and perhaps related to the practice at some other sites of covering earthern mounds with quartz or gypsum to make them stand out. A bronze axe and part of a stone one found here help to date the site.

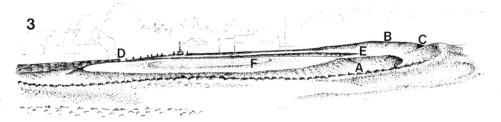

▲
King Arthur's Round Table was constructed using the easier technique of digging a ditch **A**. Like Mayburgh, however, the bank **B** rises in height towards the entrance **C**. A second entrance with two standing stones on the outside existed at **D** and inside both gaps there were causeways **E** across the ditch. Excavation showed that at the focus of these entrances there had been a small mound covering a trench with a burnt body. This mound had, however, been much destroyed by the time the present low mound **F** was built for a tea garden.

The features of both Mayburgh and the Round Table are repeated in a number of other sites known today as henge monuments. The term henge was adopted from Stone*henge* where the standing stones were erected inside an earlier circular ditched enclosure associated with pits.

Two types of henge have been recognised and both are present here: those with a single entrance (class I) and those with two entrances (class II). By analogy the Round Table should be Early Bronze Age in date with Mayburgh a little earlier. Some contemporaneity of use seems however to be implied by the bronze axe from Mayburgh. Like henges elsewhere there is the association with axes and the location by a river. Henges also tend to occur in groups and here there was a third, smaller circle to the south. Their purpose is unknown but the location by rivers suggests gatherings at focal points and in historic times the Round Table is known to have been used for games (but probably not jousting). The link with Arthur is probably early 14th century for that is the time the Cliffords became owners of nearby Brougham Castle. They claimed descent from the Welsh kings and, therefore, Arthur and it is significant that after their arrival their castle of Mallerstang became known as 'Pendragon' Castle.

Mayburgh and the Round Table are henge monuments of the late Neolithic – Early Bronze Age.

3 CASTLERIGG, KESWICK
NY 292237

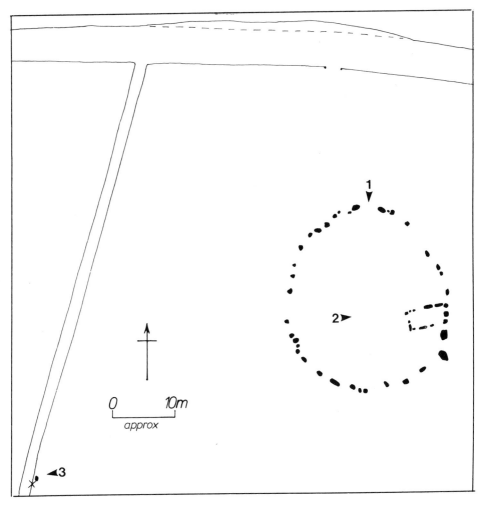

The stones of the circle appear in places to ▶ stand in a bank **A** but this is probably the headland of a ploughed area for ridge and furrow **B** runs up to it. Although the stones are of different sizes and there are gaps between them there is a definite entrance **C** formed by tall flanking stones **D** and **E** together with others placed continuously, eg **F**. The flanking stones recall those in the entrance to the henges of Mayburgh and King Arthur's Round Table.

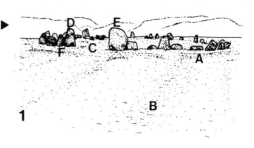

The entrance faces due north and does not have an astronomical alignment although some stones — not all the tallest — are said to be so arranged. Most astronomical and mathematical explanations for the circle fail, however, to mention the rectangle **A** which, despite some doubts about its age, can be paralleled in the centre of henges and stone circles elsewhere. The doubt expressed over the antiquity of **A** shows that without excavation the original position of no stone is certain. Equally the ▼ original environs and skyline of the site can never be known and it may be that trees obscured those parts of the present skyline which some have suggested were used for astronomical sightings. For example, if there had been more trees the height of **B** then the summit of Great Mell Fell **C** would not have been visible.

◀ Several outlying stones have been alleged to be part of the circle. This one was a large stone serving as the stile until 1915 when it was 're-erected' because it seemed to be in the right position for an 'outlier'.

The circle's purpose is unknown but it had a deliberately built entrance and rectangular area both of which can be paralleled in henge monuments with a Late Neolithic-Early Bronze Age date.

4 SHAP AVENUE
NY 560152-567133

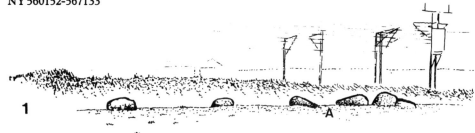

1

▲
The stones **A**, now on private land, once formed part of a site known as Karl Lofts which is
said to have been two parallel lines of stones
with their southern end a circle. Arc **A** is all
that remains of the circle and the southern part
of the site, the other stones having been broken
up by farmers or buried by the railway
embankment.

2

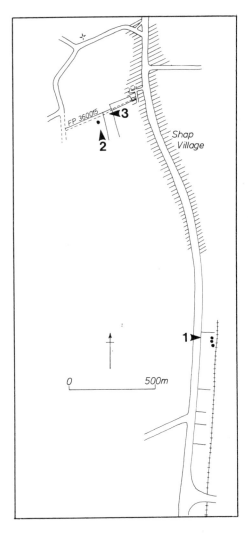

Shap
Village

0   500m

▲
Camden in the reign of Elizabeth I described
the stones to the west of the village as being of
'pyramidal form' but of these only three now
remain: a partly broken one to the south of
here, the dislodged stone **A** and the Goggleby
Stone **B**, re-erected in a concrete box after a
recent fall. Several other stones of a more
rectangular shape can be identified north west
of **A** but because their shape is different and
the alignment would have to bend sharply to
link with line **A-B** they probably formed a
separate stone row. The main avenue **A-B**
seems to have led to the circular burial mound
C, Skellaw Hill. Burial mounds and stone
circles are not uncommon ends or focal points
of other stone avenues and by analogy with
them this one is Late Neolithic-Early Bronze
Age in date. Excavation in advance of re-
erection of the Goggleby Stone found no

material which could give a closer date, but it was possible to glimpse the method of erecting this 12-ton monolith.

After digging, the hole was partly refilled with loose clay and soil. The stone was then manoeuvred until it tipped into the hole where it was held at an angle by the loose fill. In this position the effort required to haul it upright would be greatly reduced particularly if shear-legs were used. When upright the top of the hole was filled with 'packing' or wedging stones:

That stones **2A** and **2B** were only one side of an ▶ avenue is indicated by their alignment on the western side and not the centre of Skellaw Hill. The rectangular block **A** protruding either side of the wall may, therefore, represent the eastern counterpart of the Goggleby stone. The pairing of tabular stones with triangular ones is not unknown in analogous sites where the two shapes are thought to represent male and female forms. If **A** is near its original position the width of the avenue can be gauged. It will, however, be evident that the character and spacing of the stones here is very different from those at **1** so it is possible that Karl Lofts was a separate avenue.

The remains belong to two, possibly three, alignments or avenues spread over a distance of more than 1·5m (2·3km). The two identifiable ends were a stone circle and a burial mound and as elsewhere male and female forms were paired. By analogy a Late Neolithic-Early Bronze Age date can be assumed.

5 CROSBY RAVENSWORTH COMMON
NY652116-618099

NY65191164. Hollin Stump is a burial mound larger than many in the Lake District. When excavated in the 19th century nothing dateable was found but by analogy with similar sites it is Late Neolithic-Early Bronze Age in date. The only finds were a central cist containing the ▼

remains of an inhumation and, in the body of the mound, a horse's skull. This would have been a wild horse, for they were not domesticated until after the Early Bronze Age and even then seem to have been held in high esteem and not used for everyday tasks.

NY64771196. Like Hollin Stump mounds **A** and **B** were excavated by Canon Greenwell. His method of excavation was that of most of his contemporaries; a trench **C** was dug across the mound by pick and shovel the spoil being piled around, usually at one end. If nothing was found in the centre the trench was expanded until a large area was turned over, after which they gave up. Greenwell thought someone had been here first for the burial consisted of only scattered and broken bones. The stones at **D** might have been a circle or kerb and there is a hollow **E** around part of the mound. Mound **B** was said by Greenwell to have a definite kerb. There again the scattered bones of two bodies were found and in the material of the mound bones of an ox. After the building of the mound a cremation in a collared urn (see Sunbrick p 20) was inserted into it. The urn, now in the British Museum, was probably Early or Middle Bronze Age.

▼

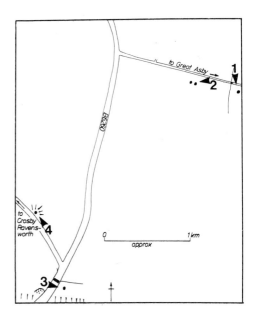

2

NY61790991. The dished centre of this mound **A** is not the result of excavation, it is an original feature. On the evidence of the few excavated examples it started as a circular bank **B** inside which burials were made. These were then sealed by filling the centre **A**. It can be described as a ring cairn.

▼

Burial mounds seem to be mainly Late Neolithic-Early Bronze Age in date. Some were simple mounds, others had external kerbs while others covered stone circles. In yet another type the circle within which the burials were placed was not formed by standing stones but by a bank. The manner of burial in all types could be either inhumation or cremation and apart from the circles there is other evidence for ritual – a horse's skull and ox bones. Perhaps there were funeral feasts.

3

▲
NY62881045. Prior to 19th-century quarrying A Penhurrock was a large cairn or mound. Its piecemeal destruction led to the uncovering of 'numerous' burials, a 'cist shaped hole' cut in the solid rock and a number of stone circles **B**. The site has been built on a natural knoll, no doubt to create an illusion of size.

6 LEVEN'S PARK RINGCAIRN
SD50568621

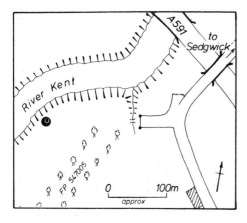

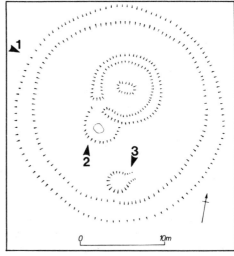

The site, now partly reconstructed, appears to have been a mound or cairn with a boulder kerb **A** sealing two earlier features with graves **B**. Alternatively **A** may have been part of a ring bank **C** inside which **B** had been constructed.
▼

As one of the graves had been built against the other the burial area had been open for some time prior to its sealing.

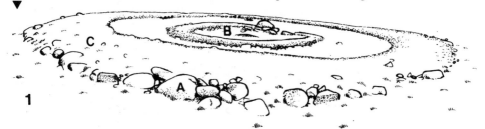

The principal internal feature was a small hut-like structure formed by a low wall **A** and an entrance **B**. The mound in its centre **C** marks the position of a plank lined grave containing a burial associated with two flint knives and 'Beaker' pottery similar to:

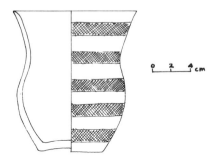

Vessels of this distinctive character can be late Neolithic or Early Bronze Age in date. The 'hut', which contained two later burials, may have been used by the dead (Beaker) person during his/her lifetime or have been a hut specially constructed for the dead or have been a ritual plan of either. Some time later, however, another burial was made beneath the large boulder **D** and covered by a low mound **E**. How long the area remained open before construction of the sealing mound is not known, but beneath all the structures were found thousands of flints of earlier date showing the funerary site had been built in an area of previous settlement.

▼

In medieval times a kiln **A** presumably for drying corn was inserted into the mound.

▼

An area of previous settlement was chosen and, perhaps delineated by a ring bank, used for burial on at least three occasions. The funerary area which included a hut-like structure was then sealed by a mound.

7 SUNBRICK STONE CIRCLE
SD28157402

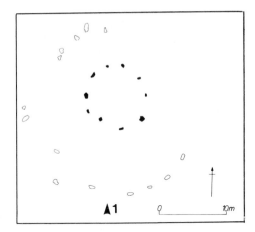

▲1

The site consists of one certain circle **A** and a possible second ring **B** not quite concentric with the first. Except for their position around **A** the limestone blocks of **B** cannot, however, be distinguished from other slabs lying on the hillside, and it is much to be regretted that the one means of checking their authenticity — the location of sockets in which they had stood — was not pursued when the site was excavated earlier this century. The excavators did, however, find 'two pavements' of erratics — one above the other — in the central area. Beneath these were two hollows with vegetable mould and a number of pits containing cremated human remains and a few stone objects such as a sandstone disc. There were two pieces of evidence for the site having been used over some length of time: the 'two' pavements were separated by an accumulation of soil and one pit had cut into another. The later pit contained an Early Bronze Age urn, now in Barrow Museum.

The urn provides a fixed date in the chronology of the site but how long the site was in use before and after its deposition cannot now be determined. The vegetable mould can be paralleled elsewhere where it has been interpreted as offerings of the fruits of the earth, eg harvest produce. The south western stones are said to be aligned on the moon, but how tall were the users of such an alignment?

▼

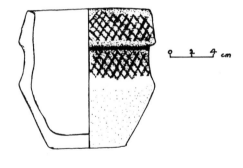

1

The site consists of one, possibly two, stone rings, and seems more ritual than astronomical. Within Cumbria there are three certain and eight other possible sites with the same characteristics: a pavement below which are one or more pits associated with cremation and Early Bronze Age objects.

20

Settlements and Hillforts

Types of Settlement

Sites such as Burwens, Sealford and Aughertree which were often labelled 'Romano British' are now called 'native settlements' in recognition that their overall shape and characteristics do not belong to a single period but are found from the Bronze Age to the post Roman period. Within native settlements the predominant building is the 'circular' hut although rectangular buildings can also be present. Some of the huts would be the equivalent of barns, others dwellings with a central hearth. Meats and dried produce were probably hung or stored in the roof space. Box type beds of the type found in the Lake District until quite recently may also have existed for they are known in the Neolithic, at Skara Brae on Orkney.

The appearance of the farmer probably changed little during prehistoric and Roman times. His appearance and the details of his plough have been preserved in a small model from Piercebridge, Durham. It shows a woollen tunic and trousers with a hood of leather, a material more waterproof than wool. The plough is of the very simple type known as an ard — a bow shaped piece with no mould

Romano-British farmer with plough

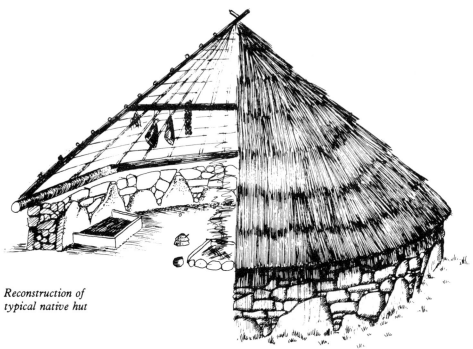

Reconstruction of typical native hut

board. It could only scratch the surface and so, to break the soil adequately, it was often necessary to replough at right angles to the first furrows. The result was square fields.

Two main types of native settlement may be recognised: those where the buildings are enclosed by a perimeter wall and those which are unenclosed. These can be further divided by the presence or absence of fields. Burwens has fields but Sealford probably did not. The unenclosed type is perhaps the earlier, for individual huts, like Levens (see p 18), are a feature of the Early Bronze Age.

The classification into different types is hindered by the fact many must be multiperiod or multiphase as at Burwens, Aughertree and perhaps Sealford. Like present farms not all the buildings would be erected at once, new ones would be added and old ones abandoned, converted or retained when necessary.

Economic need would also have influenced layout so the Iron Age pastoral farm would look more like the post Roman pastoral farm than the Iron Age arable one. Thus the western and central enclosures at Aughertree are almost impossible to date without excavation for their subrectangular shape is timeless. Similar economic needs can also lead to apparent continuity of settlement. Medieval shielings can occur alongside hillforts like Carrock Fell not because they were direct descendants but because the need for summer pasture in prehistoric and medieval times led to the exploitation of the same areas.

At Dalton dispersed farmsteads can be traced where later there was a single village and its lands. Dispersed settlement can still be found in areas of the Lake District and is obviously a 'native' pattern as much as a 'Scandinavian' one. Despite the frequent Scandinavian place names no settlement has been found which can be directly attributable to Norse farmers. It may be that having the same economy as their 'native' neighbours they built similar sites:

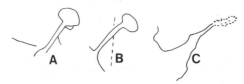

A is the 'native' settlement on Aughertree Fell, B a Norwegian medieval site and C Askham village in the 18th century. The form of all three is similar because of the provision of a drove road. Interestingly, in Norway the settlements at the ends of the droveways have been called 'tuns', an element in the names of some nucleated villages eg Dalton. A dispersed pattern of farms might therefore, lie beneath the lands of nucleated villages because that land has always been good for farming and because the village evolved from one such isolated farm. This should be no surprise for the English Place Name Society has shown how many present farmsteads have names of early origin.

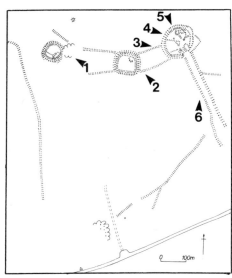

Three 'settlement enclosures' lie on this north facing hillside. In all three the material dug from the ditch has been piled inside and outside except on the uphill side, at **A**, where it is only on the inner edge. Within this western enclosure are the remains of a rectangular platform **B** and other smaller platforms, eg **C**. These platforms suggest the former existence of buildings. **D** is a quarry which has slightly damaged the site.

▼   **1**

The central enclosure with its entrance **A** is a sub-rectangular shape like the western one but has no evidence for internal buildings unless the oval depression **B** is counted. A sunken lane **C** leads towards the site. Sunken lanes were formed by a continuous process of traffic turning a hillside to mud and the mud being washed away to produce a new, fractionally lower surface, which was in turn eroded.

▼

D is probably the Bronze Age burial mound dug hereabouts in the last century. Because it was protected the unauthorised excavation was made at night and all that is known is that twelve urns were found in a circle. This suggests a circular area had been defined for burial purposes and that it was subsequently closed by the erection of a mound.

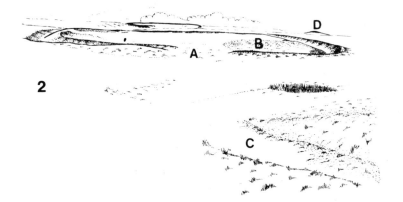

2

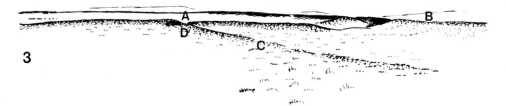

3

▲
The central enclosure is connected to the eastern one **A** by two dykes **B** and **C**. **C** cuts into the outer bank of **A** at **D** showing it was constructed later. How much later is not known.

The eastern enclosure contains building platforms, eg **A**, and is sub-divided into smaller enclosures or yards by banks such as **B**.
▼

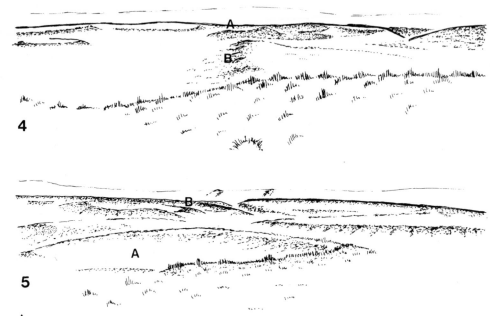

4

5

▲
Some of the buildings, such as **A**, seem to have been circular. The walls were presumably of stone although turf ones would, without excavation, now look the same particularly if built on stone foundations. The banks dividing the yards and the perimeter of the enclosure were presumably the base for stockades, hedges or fences. The whole formed a single farmstead within which some huts might replace earlier ones, new yards be created and others abandoned. The rectangular platform at **B**, for example, has been cut into the perimeter bank and must, therefore, be a late feature. The circular buildings, however, suggest a pre-medieval date.

> *At least two of the enclosures contain buildings and can, therefore, be regarded as farmsteads but the eastern one is sufficiently different to be a different date. Unlike the others it is also directly associated with a well developed system of animal management. At some time this relatively intense farming replaced or gave way to less intense land use as represented by the other enclosures and the present landscape.*

The farm's entrance **A** was approached by a very wide lane between banks **B** and **C**. Comparable features occur amongst present day fields and are droveways or *outgangs*. The provision of an embanked droveway shows it was desirable not to have animals trampling areas **E** and **F**. As there is nothing to show that such

large fields **E** and **F** were ploughed, they must have contained hay and better pasture. The droveway thus led to grazing beyond the *inbye* land. By contrast the absence of droveways to the other two enclosures **1** and **2** indicates they did not possess *inbye* land.

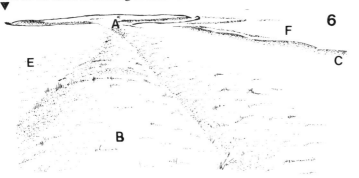

9 CARROCK FELL
NY243337

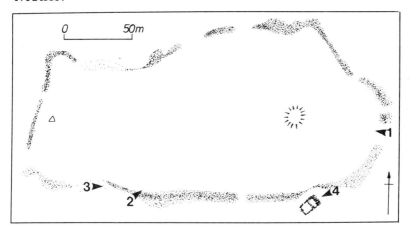

This, the largest known hillfort in Cumbria, was formed by a stone wall **A** enclosing the highest part of the ridge. There are now a number of gaps in the rampart but that at **B** is probably original ie an entrance. The neat dry stone wall **C** is a modern construction.

The original face of the wall seems, however, to ▶ survive at **A**. There is no evidence for its former height except the amount of material which has fallen from above and hidden the wall, eg at **B**. Such debris suggests a wall at least half as high again as **A**.

When the appearance of the collapsed wall at **A** ▶ is compared with **B** it will be evident that the spread of the rampart **B** cannot be natural, that the wall has been deliberately pulled down, and hillfort slighted. This act cannot be dated although the Romans have been suggested.

The cairn at **C** is ancient despite disturbance in its centre. It had the form of an Early Bronze Age burial cairn which is interesting as some hillforts elsewhere begin in the Late Bronze Age.

This relatively modern structure seems to be a sheepfold but the purpose of the narrow rectangular area **A** with its blocked entrance **B** is difficult to identify unless it is a shieling hut. The reason for the seasonal movement of men and sometimes whole families to the shielings or summer pastures is given by Denton in 1610: the barons of Burgh by Sands 'took upon them to summer their cattle there [Bewcastle] and make them shields and cabbins for their people ... because the barony itself was ... fitting better for corn and meadow than pasture'. That summer pasturing or trans-humance was widespread at an earlier time is shown by the number of place names contain-

ing the word 'scale' — Scandinavian for hut. The exposed position of some hillforts like this one may well relate to the protection of herds and flocks on the summer grounds and the huts found within such sites — but not here — could be the equivalent of shieling huts rather than permanent homes.

> *The date for the enclosure is unknown but it should be later than the burial cairn within it. The hillfort contains no visible traces of hut circles and it may simply have been in use during the summer. It was slighted at some time but by whom is not known.*

10 Burwens, Crosby Lodge
NY622123

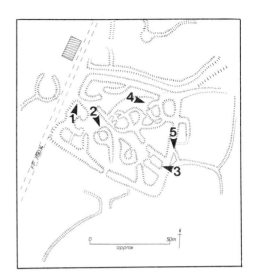

In medieval times this area was a deer park with a lodge — the latter being the origin of the present farm's name. By preventing medieval improvement of the land the park helped preserve many older landscape features including this settlement. It consists of a wall **A** surrounding a rectangular area within which are the remains of buildings, eg **B**, and yards, eg **C**. Two lanes **D** and **E** can also be traced from the single entrance **F**.
▼

Some of the buildings, eg **A** appear to be square as much as circular. None would need a central post to support the roof for their small size would allow the rafters to be self-supporting provided the latter were secured to the wall. A horizontal wallplate, not dissimilar from those in use today, was probably employed.
▼

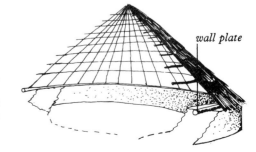

wall plate

The remains of a true rectangular building can ▶
be traced here. Like the hut circles and yards
its walls were constructed of two lines of upright slabs or orthostats **A** and **B**, the centre
being filled with earth and small stones. Dry
stone walling filled the gaps between the orthostats and was carried up to the required height.

Hut circle **A** was constructed by the same
method, the orthostats being visible at **B**. The
hut appears, however, to run beneath wall **C**, so
this corner of the settlement was remodelled at
some time.
▼

Beyond the settlement are a number of field
walls, eg **A**. There is not enough stone for them
to have been very high, even allowing for later
stone robbing, so the remains are probably
those of earthen banks or dykes supporting
fences or hedges. Field walls **B** and **C** enclose a
small area which cannot have been very
practical. It looks like the corner of a field built
over by the main enclosure **D**. **D** might, therefore, have used a field system belonging to an
earlier settlement such as that which lies to the
north. At **E** and **F** are two small grassed cairns
of the type usually called field clearance, but
whether the stones were removed for arable
use or to improve pasture is uncertain. ▶

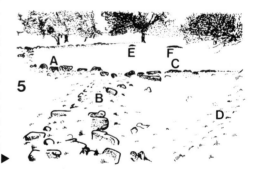

*Despite the numbers of huts and yards there is no
reason to regard the settlement as a village for
farms need more than one building. The farmstead was built in an existing agricultural landscape and at least one part was reconstructed
perhaps after the rest had been abandoned.
There is no evidence for date but rectangular
buildings such as 3A are unlikely to be prehistoric
in date, but an analogy with excavated sites
outside the Lake District could be Roman. Although there are no finds to prove it, farms like
this one must have continued into the post
Roman period and poetry supposedly composed
in 6th century Cumbria, or Rheged, does refer to
homesteads. The principal subject of the poems,
Urien Rheged, lived in Llwyvenydd which has
been equated with this valley of the Lyvennet.
Some have even identified this site with Urien's
home.*

11 THE HELM
SD531887

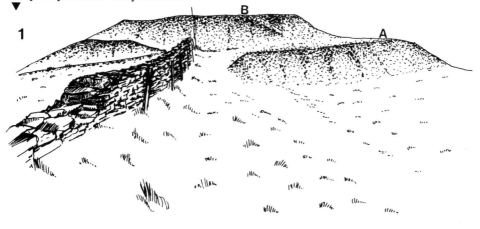

This is one of a number of hillforts on the end of a ridge. The two ramparts **A** and **B** are only on this side, steep slopes affording adequate protection everywhere else.

▼

1

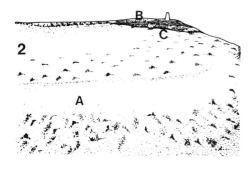

2

◀ Behind the two ramparts was a third **A** which continued around the hilltop, eg at **B**. The area this enclosed is very small but would be sufficient to hold one or two huts. The hollow **C** appears to be partly artificial and resembles a platform for a round hut. The date is unknown but a comparable site in Borrowdale yielded Roman pottery in unknown relationship to the defences.

> *This is one of a number of small hilltop enclosures of unknown date and purpose. If small farmsteads they were predominantly pastoral, for there is no evidence for ploughing around them.*

12 SEALFORD, NEAR HUTTON ROOF
SD582789

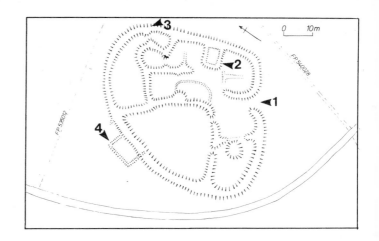

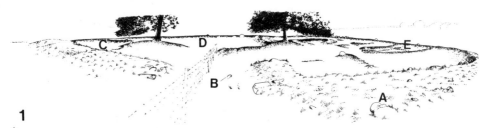

1

▲

The remains, away from the public footpath, are those of a farmstead with protecting wall **A** and single entrance **B**. Within the perimeter are a number of yards, eg **C** and **D** and some buildings eg **E**.

The two most obvious buildings are of different shapes: a rectangle **A** and circle **B**.

▼

Trench **C**, like others on the site, is the remains of early excavation. The finds were sparse but included a magnificent (tiny) bronze bull's head, probably part of a bowl. A date in the Roman period is likely for the find. A similar date for some of the buildings is suggested by the rectangular form of **A**. This may, however, be later than the rest for it was found to be better built.

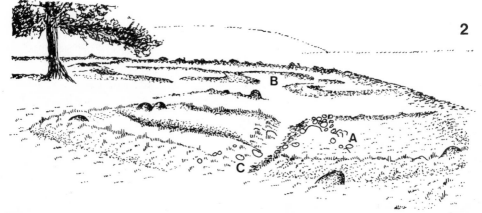

2

3

▲
Most walls consisted of two lines of uprights or orthostats **A** and **B** with small stones between and drystone walling above to the required height. What the height was cannot be determined but a low wall would have been the base for a stockade or hedge ie defence against wild animals as much as humans.

There is no evidence for contemporary fields but they may have been destroyed by later ploughing. The small enclosure **A** seems to ride over the farm's perimeter **B** representing, therefore, ancient use of the ruined or decaying farm.
▼

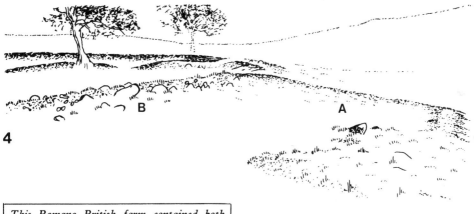

4

This Romano British farm contained both circular and rectangular buildings although not necessarily contemporaneously. If fields were absent it must have had a pastoral economy.

13 DALTON
SD544766-542754. SD542760

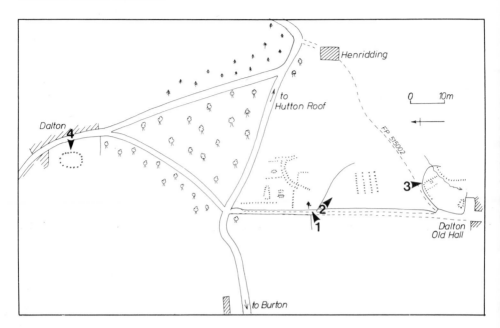

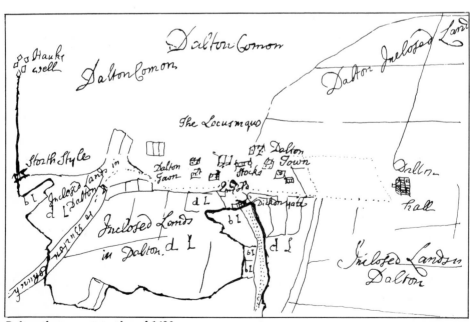

Dalton, from an estate plan of 1690

The remains are those of a deserted village with ▶ its pump **A**, lanes, eg **B**, and crofts, eg **C**. There is a late 19th-century story that it was deserted after the Black Death, but if there was any truth in this it either refers to a different site or the village had been re-established by 1690 when it is shown on an estate plan.

The plan shows a thriving village with its stocks where the present Hutton Roof-Burton road now runs. The village is again shown on the Tithe Map of 1820 but had gone by the time of the first Ordnance Survey map (1847). Why it disappeared is not known. Perhaps the estate was remodelled and the tenants were given new houses further north, perhaps it was the victim of population drift to the industrial towns for the rural population of the county decreased dramatically in the early 19th century.

Between the village and the Old Hall at **A** is an area of early arable fields **B**. The steps are called 'strip lynchets' and have been caused by the plough cutting into the hillside. As the ploughing on each step must have been done separately from that on the next, each strip may have belonged to a different person ie they are the remains of the village field, separated from the latter by wall **C**. At **D** the faint traces of more strips are overlain by **C** as if the latter and, therefore, part of the village is later than the lynchets.
▼

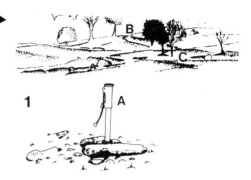

1

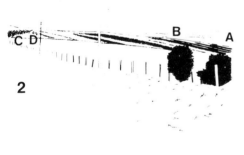

SD542754 The present footpath is the direct descendant of the old lane **A**. Beyond are vestiges of a rectangular building **B** with a yard **C**. These remains seem to be those of a farm but they are too close to the Old Hall to be contemporary and so must be earlier.
▼

3

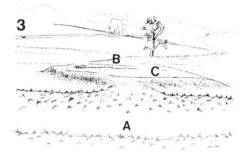

SD544766 The oval of boulders **A** may be the site referred to in the story of the Black Death. Although it looks like the village pound with its pump **B** it does not appear on the map of 1690. It must, therefore, be an earlier site re-used by **B**. Its form is that of a pre-medieval farm such as Sealford.
▼

2

4

The village seems to overlie the remains of an earlier landscape of scattered farmsteads. Parts of the earlier farms, their boundaries and lanes seem to have been retained by the later village and the name itself (Dalton) suggests it grew from one such farm.

Roman Forts

The Development and Arrangement of Roman Forts

First century forts, as at Ambleside, were of turf and timber but from the reign of Trajan (98-117 AD) onwards stone walls became the norm. Under Hadrian the fort attained its textbook form which was rigidly applied at both Ambleside and Hardknott to tactical disadvantage.

The Hadrianic fort in the North of England was usually square or rectangular in plan with rounded corners and gateways in the centre of each wall. The gates were hinged by vertical irons pivoted in the ground and in the arch or lintel. Each gateway had one or two passageways depending upon the volume of traffic and was carried one storey above the height of the curtain wall as were the towers at the corners. The curtain wall had a rampart bank behind to give greater strength and in front there was a ditch, unless natural slopes afforded adequate protection. Where the lie of the land weakened the fort's defences the number of ditches was increased. The headquarters building with its courtyard, crosshall and shrine was at the intersection of the roads between the gates. On either side were the granaries and command-ant's house and examples elsewhere show that a hospital was also part of this central group. At both Hardknott and Ambleside only the three main buildings were of stone the others, barracks and workshops, being of timber or half timber construction. The commandant would have his own bath suite but that for ordinary soldiers was outside the fort presumably because it was too cramped inside.

The forts were usually designed to hold full auxiliary regiments, or cohorts, of about five hundred men. The auxiliaries were drawn from amongst non-citizens of the Empire, those at Hardknott coming from Dalmatia in modern Yugoslavia. At Hardknott, however, the evidence suggests a full cohort was not in permanent garrison and the first fort at Ambleside was too small for a full unit. It is dangerous, therefore, to assume the number of forts equals the number of regiments deployed or that all known forts were in contemporary use. Some forts like Hardknott would be abandoned and new ones created as the situation required. The number and quality of excavations do not, unfortunately, allow us to reconstruct the complete Roman military disposition at any one time.

Schematic plan of a Roman fort

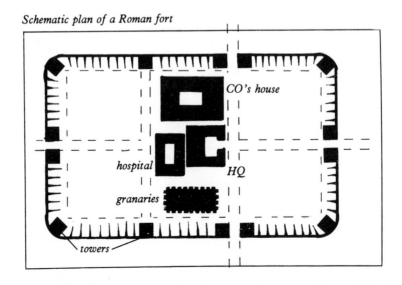

CO's house

hospital

HQ

granaries

towers

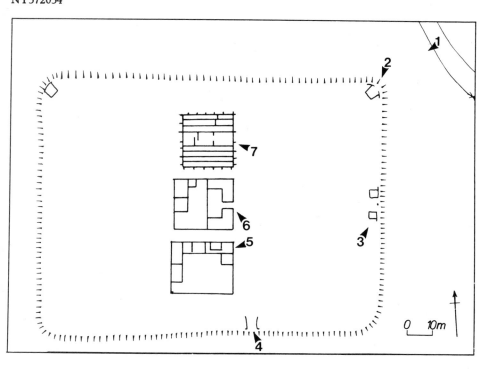

The fort is visible as a rectangular platform **A** at the head of Lake Windermere. The exact position of the water's edge in Roman times is not known but the River Rothay **B** and the Lake must have afforded adequate protection to the south and west for only on the northern and eastern sides were ditches **C** added to the defences. The effect of the double ditch was, however, lessened by the rocky knoll **D** being beyond.

1

2

▲
The curtain wall **A** and **B** had a round corner behind which was a square tower **C**. The excavators found the tower had gone out of use in the Roman period and had been replaced by a building with a slate roof.

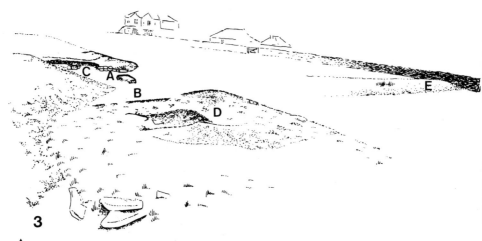

3

▲
In the centre of each side was a gate, this one having two passageways **A** and **B** with flanking guardrooms **C** and **D**. Behind the curtain wall was an earthen rampart which butted up against the sides of the guardrooms and corner turrets, both of which would be carried one storey above the height of the curtain.

E is the causeway of the road running eastwards from the gate. To its north and presumably served by roads linking with it was the civil settlement or *vicus* which grew up around the fort. The *vicus* would start with traders and service industries relieving the soldiers of their pay. With them would come women and children forming a community in which the soldiers, in good time, could establish their own roots.

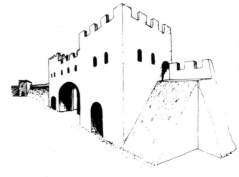

The cemetery of both *vicus* and fort was further east.

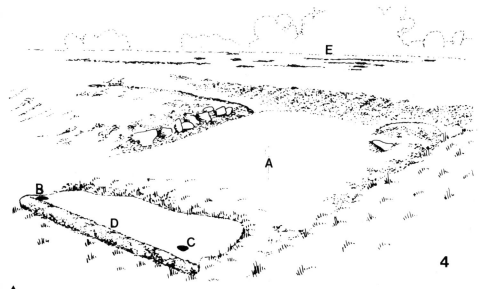

▲
The south gate had only a single passage **A** presumably because proximity to the lake caused little traffic. The pivot holes **B** and **C** show there were two doors which opened inwards and shut against the ridge **D**. There was no flanking guard chamber(s) so one must have been provided in the tower above the passageway. It would have been reached via the curtain and from steps in the back of the rampart. West of the road connecting this gate with the northern one were the principal buildings **E**. These were of stone with the other buildings, barracks and workshops, being of timber.

The commandant's house consisted of a series of rooms, eg **A**, around a central courtyard **B**. This design was derived from city houses in Italy where rooms looked inwards towards a shady courtyard and away from the crowded, noisy streets outside.
▼

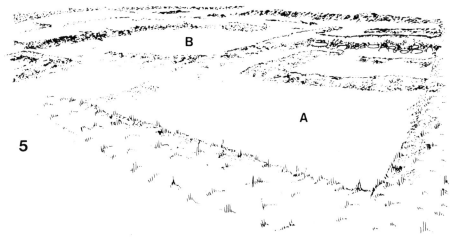

The headquarters or *principia* was also built ▶ around a courtyard **A** in the centre of which was found a stone block, presumably for a statue. The small rooms, eg **B**, on three sides of the courtyard were for stores, equipment etc. The fourth side was a hall **C** the full-length of the building. In the hall the commanding officer carried out disciplinary hearings and regimental administration. The focus of regimental life was, however, the small shrine, room **D**, where the standards were kept. Beneath is a strong room for the pay chests. The shrine was so positioned that it could be seen through the entrance of the great hall, through the entrance to the courtyard **E** and through the principal gateway, here at **3**.

Finds from the excavations show the stone buildings were erected during the reign of Hadrian and that the hall was slated and glazed. The walls at **F** were also found to have subsided into an earlier double ditch in which the strongroom had been built. These ditches belonged to an earlier fort which was not rectangular in plan. It had timber buildings and a turf wall and rampart on a pavement of slabs. Unlike the later fort it took in knoll **D**.

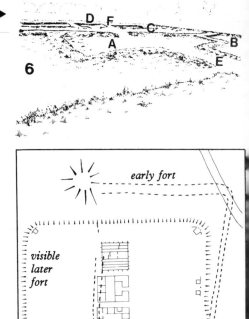

6

early fort

visible later fort

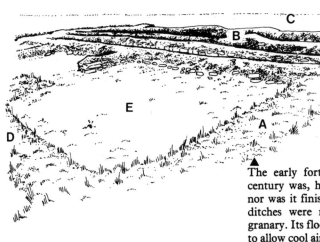

7

A Hadrianic fort with walls, towers and principal buildings of stone replaced an earlier turf-built one of sub-rectangular design. The excavators found no evidence for occupation through to the end of the Roman period although the north eastern tower had been drastically altered at some time.

The early fort, built at the end of the 1st century was, however, not occupied for long nor was it finished for beneath building **A** its ditches were missing, not dug. **A** was the granary. Its floor was raised on low walls, eg **B**, to allow cool air to circulate underneath. There were two main floors **C** and **D** separated by a passage **E**. As the external buttressed wall continues across **E** the building must have had a single roof, probably with gables over **C** and **D** and a valley above **E**. The first period granaries had been a little further east. They were smaller, for their fort was smaller, but quantities of charred wheat survived.

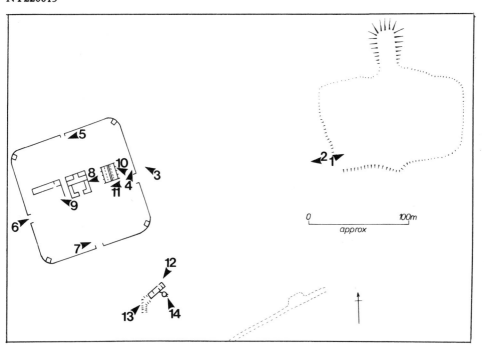

North east of the fort is the parade ground, a level area **A** of approximately three acres. Although the mountain side here is less steep than elsewhere the surface of **A** is artificial, the ground having been dug out at **B** and built up at **C** and **D**. The heap of stones **E** is the officer's platform and opposite, at **F** is a small projection presumably for some item connected with regimental ceremonial.
▼

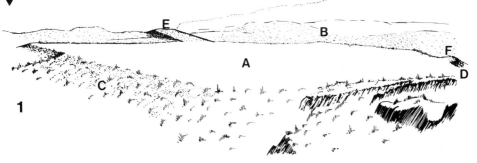

The fort **A** is sited on a spur between the valleys of the Hardknott Gill **B** and River Esk **C**. Where the Esk enters the sea at Ravenglass there was another fort and a third was located the same distance to the east at Ambleside. At Hardknott the fort was laid out regardless of terrain as a square with rounded corners and a gateway in the centre of each side.

At each corner of the fort was an internal tower **A**. This rose one storey above the adjacent wall top which was approximately three times its present height. As this side of the fort was, however, overlooked by higher ground it was given the added protection of two ditches **B** and **C**.

The walls have been consolidated by the Department of the Environment. Below the course of thin slabs **D** the stones are as they were in Roman times. They were saved from later stone robbers by having been buried by masonry fallen from above. Above **D** the walls have been partly rebuilt using some of that fallen stonework.

The outside of the curtain wall was faced with squared blocks of local stone, eg **A**, but the inner side was left rough **B** because it would be hidden by a rampart bank. At each gateway the ends of the bank were revetted with masonry **C**. The occurrence of two faces **D** and **E** in the entrance passage is explained by the curtain being built first, with the rampart and its revetting added slightly later.

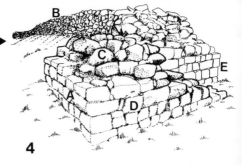

5

▲ All the gateways except this one were wide enough for two passageways. Here, where the ground at **A** becomes a cliff, few would need to come and go and a single portal was sufficient. Recess **B** may indicate the arched entrance was set back from the face of the curtain but more probably held the jambs against which the doors shut and for which there is no other evidence. The neat end of the curtain implies the jambs were added later like the revetting. The disappearance of the jambs must be attributable to them being of imported freestone (robbed by local builders).

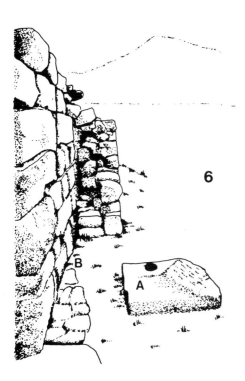

6

◄ The pivot stone for one of the doors **A** shows the freestone was red sandstone. **A** may, however, not be in its original position for it is not worn, either it is a brand new replacement or it is the pivot from above the door. The recess **B** may be explained by later robbing of freestone jambs. If so the absence of similar recesses at the rear of the gate implies the vaulted passageways were of local rock with only the front arches of sandstone.

The southern gate does, however, seem to have ▶ had rear arches of sandstone for the base of the pillar between them **A** is of that rock and the quoins at **B** have been robbed. This gateway is also different from the others in having the revetting **C** flush with the curtain. These differences are explained by its being the main entrance to the fort. Fragments of an inscription originally set between its arches were found during excavation. The inscription, now in Carlisle Museum, records the building of the fort under Hadrian c130 by the 4th cohort of Dalmatians. This gateway, like the others, would be continued above parapet height as a tower. It presumably contained the guardroom entered from the curtain wall.

7

B

C

A

The road through the main gate led to the entrance **A** of the *principia* or headquarters building. **A** opened into a courtyard **B** around which were rooms **C** and **D** containing offices and armouries. On the opposite side to **A** was a hall **E** the full length of the building. Here the commanding officer carried out his duties and the supporting wall for his tribunal survives at **F**. Down the side of the hall were two more offices **G** and **H** either side of the shrine of the standards **I**. As the shrine was the centre of the fort's and regiment's life it was so positioned that it could be seen through the door into the hall, through **A** and from the main gate. The thinness of the walls of the *principia* suggests the upper part was half timbered. It was roofed with tiles and had glazed windows.
▼

8

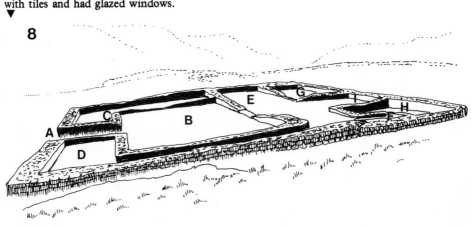

The commandant's house or *praetorium* was ▶
also planned around a courtyard **A** and the
thinness of the walls again implies a half
timbered superstructure. The sudden end of
wall **B** may indicate that the remainder of the
building was wholly timber framed or, more
likely, that it was never finished. On the other
hand early excavators found boxtiles —
normally associated with hypocaust systems —
in wing **C** suggesting that that range of rooms
was completed.

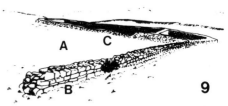

9

10

▲
The floor of the granary was raised on pillars
A to allow cool air to circulate underneath. It
has been estimated that the building could
hold more than three hundred tons or enough
grain to supply the regiment (500 men) for two
years. Although under one roof there were in
fact two granaries separated by wall **B**. Pillars

A were originally in the centre of the eastern
granary but acquired their present asym-
metrical appearance when wall **C** was inserted.
This new wall could have been connected with
a re-roofing and in particular the provision of
two separate pitched roofs with a central
valley.

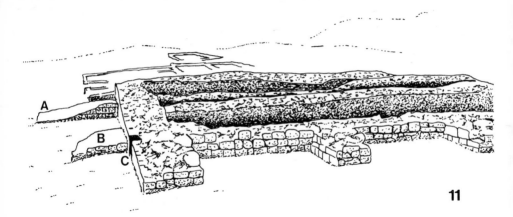

11

The ramps to facilitate loading of the two granaries have survived **A** and **B** but an odd feature of the building is the absence of vents to aid air circulation beneath the floor. It is, however, possible that the blocked holes either side of each ramp, eg **C**, performed this function. If so their blocking means new vents were provided at a higher level or that the use of the building was changed.

Note that only the three principal buildings had stone walls. The barracks and workshops which should have filled the remainder of the fort must have been of timber.

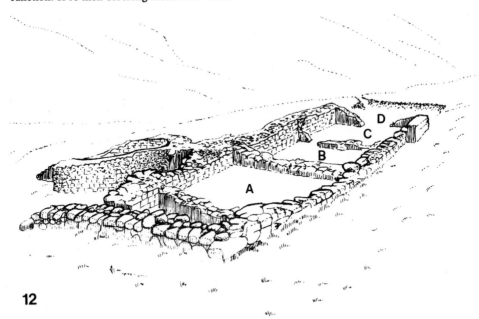

12

The bathhouse outside the fort's walls was simple and small. It is difficult to believe it served a full cohort. The three principal rooms were the cold plunge (*frigidarium*) **A**, warm bath (*tepidarium*) **B** and hot bath (*caldarium*) **C**. The gaps in the wall between **B** and **C** allowed the passage of hot air beneath the floor. The furnace for this was at **D** with the *caldarium* next to it to obtain maximum heat.

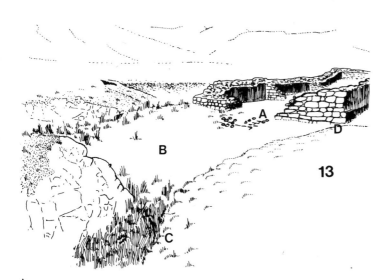

▲
The furnace, at **A**, was brick built and located in a sunken or sheltered area **B**. Channel **C** formerly containing a lead pipe in concrete was cut to drain that area and also carry surplus water from the baths. This end of the building was, however, rebuilt at some stage for it incorporates freestone blocks, eg **D**, which must have come from some (important) demolished structure.

The *Laconicum* (sauna type bath) was heated through **A**. The butt joint **B** shows it too was altered.
▼

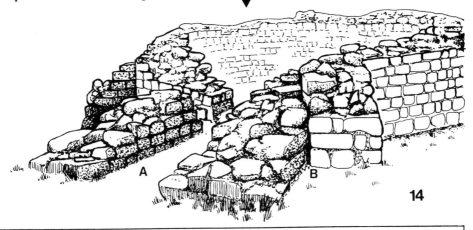

This Hadrianic fort ostensibly guarded the road inland from Ravenglass but the size of the bathhouse suggests there was never a full regiment in permanent garrison. The half completed commandant's house suggests the fort was intended to hold a full regiment but that the decision to reduce its strength was taken before building work was finished. The junior officer now in command had a status and social needs requiring only the one suite of rooms. It is tempting to link this reduction in manpower to the Romans' need to find troops for the re-occupation of Southern Scotland in 146. Even though they subsequently withdrew from there the need for this fort can never have been great and there is no evidence for occupation beyond 250 AD.

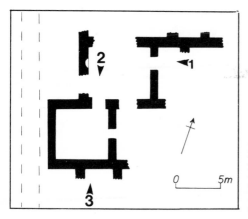

Despite the name the remains are those of a Roman building east of the largely destroyed Roman fort. The niche **A** is reminiscent of those in the changing room of the bathhouse at Chesters on Hadrian's Wall so room **B** and the building has been interpreted as having a similar function. It had a solid floor unlike **C** which contained a hypocaust. Between **B** and **C** was an anteroom formed by wall **D** and lit by window **E**. The latter appears to have been blocked in Roman times.

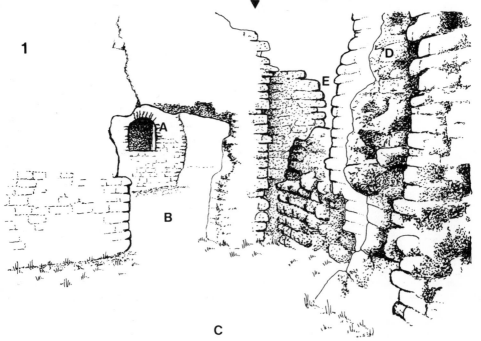

The room at **A** was lit by a window **B** the same ▶ height as **1E**. The room, which gave access to another with a hypocaust, has a very worn threshold **C** with a broad groove down each side. By analogy with other sites these grooves held stone (slab) door jambs; stone being preferred to wood in the steamy atmosphere.

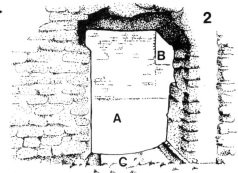

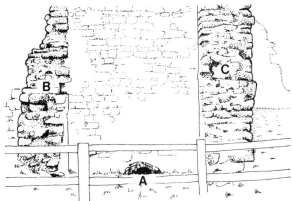

▲
The solid floor of room **2A** replaced an earlier one with a hypocaust heated through the blocked flue **A**. The walls **B** and **C** indicate a room or screen existed here but like much of the building its character and extent has not yet been determined.

The lack of early excavation is fortunate for it would have missed the evidence, if any, for post Roman use. One suggestion is that the building formed the manor house of the Penningtons prior to their removal to Muncaster, another that it served as the Leper hospital known to have been in this area. More tantalising, however, are two traditions recorded in the late 16th — early 17th centuries. In one the remains were called 'Lyons Garde' a name derived from a celtic divinity, the Lady of the Fountain. In a late Welsh poem she was the wife of Owen, son of Urien Rheged ruler of the post Roman kingdom based on the northern part of Cumbria. In Malory's poem Morte D'Arthur 'Lyons Garde' became Castle Perilous beside the Isle of Avalon. The other late 16th century tradition was that a king Eveling lived here and, as W. G. Collingwood

showed, he was Evelac or Avallach the celtic Lord of the Underworld. By Malory's time his name and attributes had become a place, a blessed isle, Avalon. But the link between the two traditions does not end there for in mythology Avallach was related to Morgan, another water goddess, who was sometmes said to be the mother of Mabon identified with Owen Rheged. While both traditions may be variants of the same story or fiction it would seem celtic mythology survived in Cumbria until quite recently. This is all the more remarkable since Ravenglass is in an area with numerous 'Scandinavian' place names. Behind the mythology there may, however, be the memory of an actual marriage alliance between this area and Rheged. In this context it is worth noting that the medieval barony of Egremont does seem to have been a semi-independent area until the 12th century.

> *The remains are those of the most upstanding Roman building in the North of England and perhaps for that reason attracted or retained a most curious and exciting legend.*

Castles and Fortified Buildings

The Englishman's Home is his Castle: Castles in General

Brougham castle combined strength with residential accommodation for castles were fortified buildings, the majority being residences. Thus the only distinction between 'castles' and 'fortified manor house' is the degree of fortification and not surprisingly medieval writers often used the term 'castle' loosely. As a residence of the martial classes the castle was also a base for military activity and, therefore, the target for attack. In well defended sites, however, the military balance was in favour of the defenders if food and water supplies were secure. Thus in the siege of Carlisle in 1315 the Lanercost Chronicle records only one Englishman dead but numerous Scots.

The strongest and earliest castles were those erected by the king and his barons (Carlisle, Brougham, Egremont and Kendal). In their earliest form these were earthwork and timber structures with a bailey and citadel. Two types

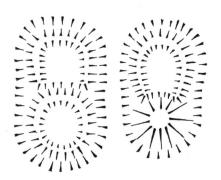

Ring work & bailey   Motte and bailey

can be recognised: bailey and motte, eg Kendal's Castle How and Egremont, and the bailey and/or ring work, eg Carlisle (and Appleby). Interestingly at Aldingham (not accessible to the public) the motte was a reconstructed ring work. There was a tendency in the 12th century for these castles to be

rebuilt in stone with a great tower or keep as the new citadel. The latest of these keeps was at the brand new castle of Brougham c1203 where the courtyard was the equivalent of the bailey and surrounded the keep like a ringwork. By that time, however, the great keep was no longer considered an absolute necessity and at the near contemporary castle of Kendal the plan is basically that of the ringwork alone. Nevertheless the word 'keep' continued to be used of a principal tower, the 1572 survey of Kendal castle referring to a 'keep' there. By contrast the gateway, originally a simple tower as at Egremont, increased in strength either by the addition of a barbican (Carlisle) or the use of flanking towers (Kendal). There and at Brougham the gatehouse was part of the main accommodation block.

The lesser castles appear to be 14th and 15th century in date and built by manorial lords as a response to Scottish raids. Three main types may be recognised. The rectangular or symmetrical castle (Penrith and Millom), the tower either by itself (Arnside) or attached to an existing house (Clifton) and the manor house and associated buildings with curtain wall appended as at Beetham (visible from the A6 at SD499790). A little explored question is what manorial accommodation preceded such fortifications. At Millom there is the hint of a fortified moated site and at Beetham there is a reference in 1255 to 'the hall...and houses within the court'. A number of pele-towers near small moats eg Whitehall (NY203413) where both are visible from the A595. As it would seem sensible to build the pele inside the moat the tower must have been added to an existing house which had replaced the moat at an earlier time. With time the need for the individual to defend his home lessened and the residential element became dominant with fortifications purely decorative. The functional castle became the 'great house' or 'stately home', but then that is what they always had been.

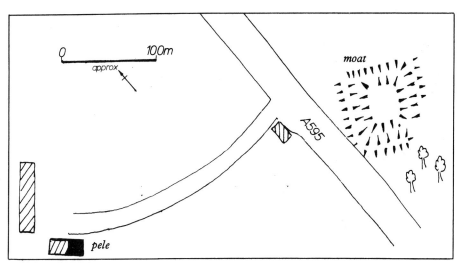

*Beetham Hall
from the A6*

Whitehall

1

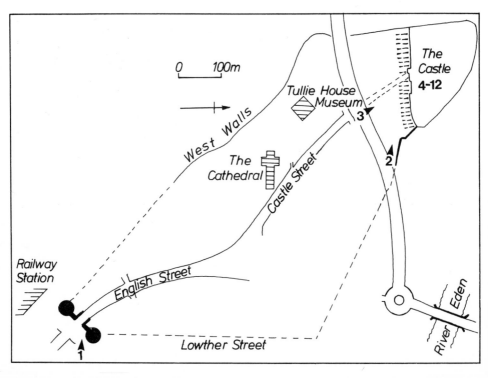

◀ At the south end of the city is the 'citadel'. The present buildings begun in 1810 replaced a fort built by Henry VIII:

1a

▲
The fort was designed to carry guns in the embrasures **A** and on the 'roof'. Inside were two 'houses' and at the rear another battery commanding the city and its walls. As the medieval city-gate **B** was incorporated into the fort and its portal **C** walled up it was necessary to provide a new gate. Known as the English Gate this was built north of tower **D**. Henry's German engineers planned similar artillery forts at other points around the city and castle, but they seem never to have been completed.

This is the only portion of the city wall visible on the eastern side. Its neat blocks are almost certainly Roman, quarried from either Hadrian's Wall or ruins in the city. Consequently it has always been difficult to distinguish the medieval city wall from the Roman one inferred to have existed from the account of St Cuthbert's visit c685. Similarly the bridge carrying the A6 over the Eden just to the east of here is the latest of a series of structures going back to Roman times. The castle **A** was built at this end of the city to command the crossing.
▼

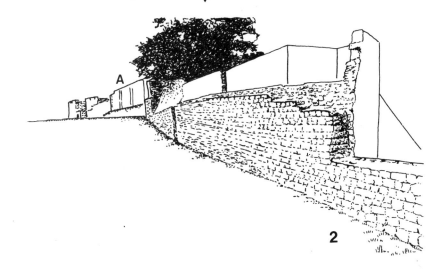

2

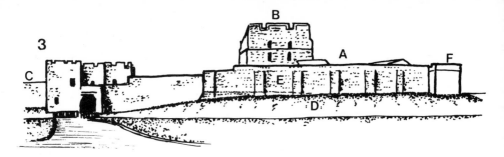

3

The castle consists of an inner bailey **A** with keep **B** and an outer bailey **C**. Both baileys stand on low mounds, eg **D**, indicating earth and timber predecessors. The first structure was built by William II in 1092 when the Normans annexed Cumberland, previously under Scottish rule. The speed with which a timber castle could be constructed is indicated by the entry in the *Anglo Saxon Chronicle*: 'In

this year King William . . . built and garrisoned the castle with his men'. Thereafter it was to remain a Royal castle. The rebuilding in stone was probably begun c1120 when Henry I ordered the city to be fortified with a castle and towers. Wall **E** with its pilasters belongs to that time as perhaps does the keep. The top of wall **E** is, however, later as is the masonry **F** which blocks an earlier gate.

4

The main gatehouse, parts of which may date from 1168, was approached by a drawbridge at **A**. When raised the bridge fitted into the

rectangular recess **B** closing the entrance to the barbican **C**. Postern **D** gave access to 'the Ladies walk' **E**.

Beyond the raised drawbridge the entrance ▶
was defended by the barbican **A**, a portcullis **B**
and gates at the front and rear of the passage.
The barbican allowed defenders at **C** to fire on
the backs of those trying to break through the
portcullis and gates.

5

Once through the outer gate attackers would
come under fire from the inner bailey **A** and, if
still held, wall top **B** and gate tower **C**. Bridge
D replaces a drawbridge deliberately positioned within close range of **A**, **B** and **C**. The
ditches originally contained water and were
stocked like fish ponds. The half moon battery
E is obviously later but the position of its
embrasures shows the present surface of the
outer bailey is higher than the ancient one. The
buildings in the bailey are 18th and 19th
century but amongst those mentioned in 1255
as being here were granges, stables, bakeries
and breweries.
▼

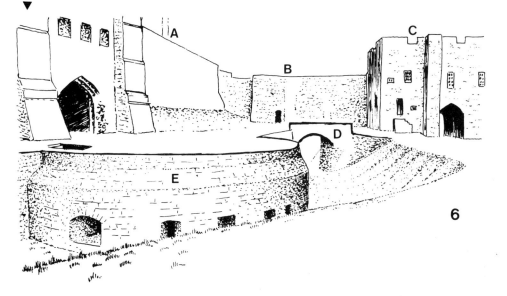

6

Another barbican defended the entrance to the ▶
inner bailey. The top of its walls **A** and **B**,
demolished prior to construction of the battery
6E, was reached through door **C**.

▲
The inner bailey, like the outer one, contained
a number of buildings other than the keep.
Chief of these was the 'palace' built by Edward
I who used Carlisle as the base for his Scottish
wars and who, as a consequence, had three
parliaments meet here. The tower to the east of
the site of the palace — parts of which may
survive in the museum block — contained a
gate defended by a portcullis in slot **A**. The
new masonry **B** is that observed at **3F**. Postern
C opened onto 'the Ladies Walk' **4E**.

The present entrance to the keep was defended ▶
by a portcullis in **A** but the original doorway
was at first floor level behind building **B**.
There is no evidence for an external staircase or
building covering such stairs as was usual but
access by ladder seems improbable. Foundations **C** must be part of a forecourt building
but contemporary with the present doorway as
offset **D** is opposite. The present entrance is
attributed to Edward I.

54

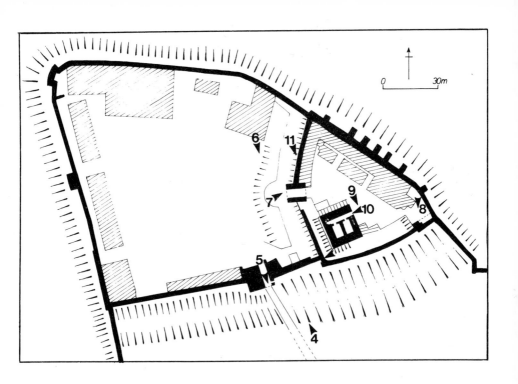

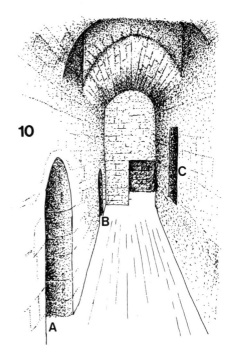

Two pairs of rooms **A** and **B** are separated by a wall which rises the full height of the keep. This part of the basement was originally lit by window **C** now blocked on the outside.

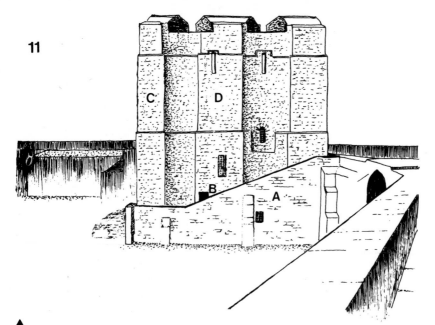

11

▲
The window **10C** was blocked when staircase **A** was built. The shallow angle of this staircase is best explained by it serving as a ramp to haul heavy weapons on to the adjacent ramparts. These were altered by Henry VIII to carry artillery and Cromwell similarly amended the keep in 1648. As early as 1384, however, two great 'gunnes' were mounted on the keep with a lesser one in the angle of the outer bailey. These primitive bronze cannons firing stone

12

ordnance were mounted on wooden frames and bound with iron. They cannot have been very effective and would have supplemented the traditional artillery or 'engines' (see **12** below) which are recorded from time to time as being within or being constructed at the castle. Staircase **A** would be admirably suited for hauling either 'engines' or 'guns'. Whenever it was constructed the well in the thickness of the keep's wall was opened up **B**.

Although much amended the keep still possesses Norman characteristics — approximately square in plan with (now recased) corner and central pilasters **C** and **D**. Its position allowed it to command both the inner bailey and the ground outside the castle. Its building is usually attributed to King David who occupied Carlisle when Stephen allowed Cumberland to return to Scottish hands.

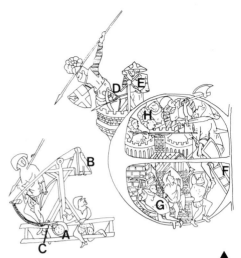

◀ From the inner bailey it was possible to command the walls of the outer one **A**, and embrasure **B** is sufficiently wide to cover both the inside and outside of the castle. Beyond the moat was an open area and the city ditch approximately on the line of the now widened road **C**. At **D** excavation has revealed the southern rampart of an early Roman fort built like the castle to command a river crossing. Beyond the west wall of that fort and the city **E** is the river Caldew. The castle and city are thus sited on a defendable ridge at the crossing of the Eden. At **F** was the medieval Caldewgate, the principal point of Scottish attack in 1315. A contemporary account of the siege survives and it is illustrated in the initial letter of Edward II's charter to the city:

'On the 5th day of the siege they set up a machine for casting stone...against the Caldewgate....' This engine or *mangonel* had a sling at one end **A** and a counterweight **B** at the other. The sling was held by a pin **C** which when knocked out by the man to the right allowed the counterweight to swing down hurling the stone through the air. '... But there

were seven or eight similar engines within the city, besides other engines...called *springgalds*, for discharging long darts....' This type of gun **D** sometimes known as a *ballista* was basically a large cross bow tensioned by being wound back **E**. '...Meanwhile, however, the Scots set up a certain great *bere frai* like a kind of tower, which was considerably higher than the city walls....' but it stuck in wet ground before reaching its destination. Mobile towers of this kind allowed the attackers to fire down on the defenders, and their own men to scale the unprotected walls under the cover of its sides. '...Moreover the Scots had made many long ladders [**F**] also a sow for mining the town wall.' A miner such as **G** was vulnerable to missiles from above **H** and, therefore, a 'sow' or roof wheeled up to the walls at the point of mining was employed. In the drawing the 'sow' is omitted, the miner, with medieval humour (?), being knocked flat with a stone on the back of his head.

In Roman and Medieval times Carlisle's geographical position caused it to be a frontier stronghold. Frequently visited by armies of one side or another – the last Scottish occupation by force was in 1745 – there was always a need to repair, patch and modernise its defences. The demolition of medieval buildings to make way for 18th and 19th-century barracks and their retention by the army today shows that certain military factors do not change even if the weaponry does.

18 PENRITH CASTLE

NY513299

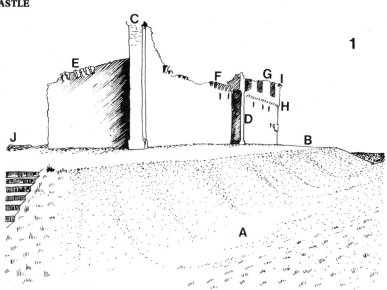

1

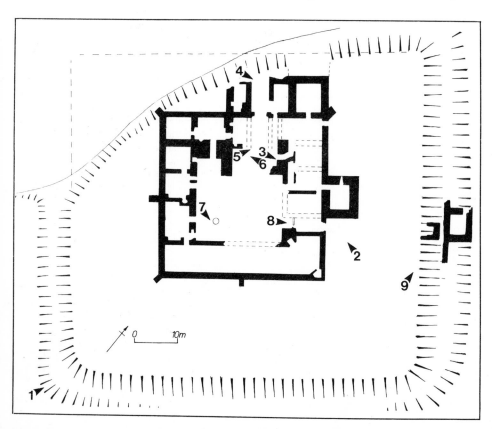

The castle situated on a hilltop overlooking the town, was protected by a ditch **A** separated from the walls by a wide space **B**. The reason for **B** is not clear but at Norham (Northumberland) the local population protected their animals from raiders by simply herding them within the ditches. Area **B** may have served a similar purpose. The main part of the castle is basically square in plan with originally diagonal buttresses, eg **C**, at three corners. Three of the walls also had central buttresses, eg **D**. The buttresses were continued above the adjacent battlements as turrets. The battlements projected on massive corbels **E** and **F** so that missiles could be dropped without exposing the defenders (machiolation). At the eastern corner was an extra storey **G** carried on small corbels **H** with the machiolation above **I**. Little survives of the west corner **J** which fell c1750.

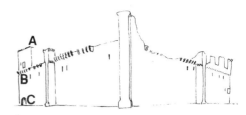

This reconstruction of the view prior to 1750 is based upon a drawing of 1739. The tower **A** cannot have been original for the machiolation **B** shows battlements once existed. A postern **C** was also visible in 1739.

The earliest part of the castle is tower **A** but only the lowest part is original. The smaller stonework **B** set back from the face of the bigger blocks is 20th century. The tower which gave flanking fire to gate **C** was begun in white stone, only a little of which occurs elsewhere in the castle and then largely either side of **A**. Plinth **D**, for example, begins white and becomes red **E**. This may be explained by surviving documents. In 1397 a cleric, William Strickland, was licensed to erect a fortified 'chamber' and a further licence in 1399 provided for its extension by a 'mantlet of stone and lime' to give 'succour' to the town. Between these two dates he was given permission to quarry stone on the nearby fell. It seems that he began his 'chamber' or tower in white stone but, before building was far advanced, decided to construct the square enclosure which forms most of the present castle. With those white stones not yet used he began building on either side of the tower, eg at **D**, and when they were finished continued in red sandstone **E** from the new quarry.

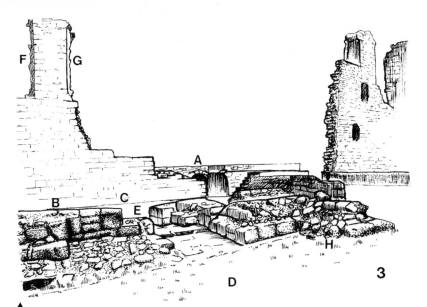

3

▲ Beneath Strickland's tower was a vault **A** now reconstructed. Red stonework **B** continuing that begun in white **C** is again evident. Between the courtyard **D** and the mantlet were various rooms, eg **E**. A survey of the derelict castle in 1572 lists three stables, chapel, great chamber, great hall, two kitchens, bakehouse, brewhouse and offices. The great hall was probably above **E**, two of its three windows **F** and **G** surviving. Stonework **H** built against the hall has been interpreted as a ramp to stables along the north west side of the castle.

Butt joint **A** shows the 'Red Tower' **B** has been added to Strickland's mantlet **C**. Plinth **D** shows the tower's side wall was intended to be external so guard chambers **E** and **F** and the entrance between **G** are even later additions. Prior to that extension there was a gate at **H** secured by a drawbar in hole **I**. The new gate was protected by a portcullis in slot **J**. As the face of the Red Tower at **K** continues well below ground level it must have formed one side of the ditch across which there was probably a drawbridge.

▼

4

5

The date of postern **A** is uncertain but door **B** belongs to the basement of the Red Tower **C**. The main gate **D** opened into a passage between walls **E** and **F**. This internal barbican with a portcullis at its inner end was replaced by the new gate passage **G** (**4G**).

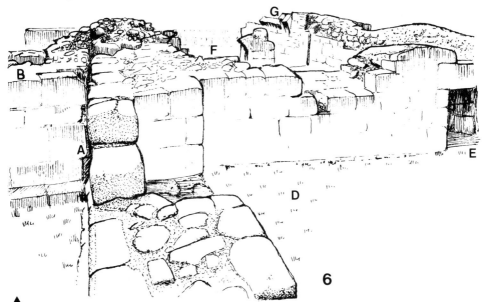

6

The butt joint **A** shows **B** is later than the buildings behind the mantlet. It was probably another ramp like **3H**. Examination of the walls of the buildings around the courtyard will, however, reveal they in turn are butted against the mantlet. Room **D** possessed a fireplace **E** while those at **F** were vaulted **G**.

7

8   A

        B

62

◀The floor joists of this range were either bedded into the wall, eg **A**, or rested on corbels **B**. The windows **C** and fireplaces, eg **D**, imply both upper floors were for occupation. At **E** are the remains of a kiln said to be for smoking meat while the large window above, **F**, was probably the east window of the chapel. The chapel represents a modification of this corner, its stonework **G** being different from that below.

9

▲
The stonework in the ditch is not easily interpreted but **A** looks like a bridge abutment with wall **B** forming a vertical inner face of the ditch. **C** must be a tower, allowing the remains to be identified with the 'outer gatehouse' described in 1572 as being in 'utter ruin'.

The castle whose owners included (the later) Richard III was begun in 1397-9 as a tower on one side of a square mantlet in which there were probably two gateways and two posterns. 'Mantlet' means screen and its purpose must have been just that, to screen those within from raiders. The ditch seems to have served a similar purpose. Shortly after 1399, perhaps before the mantlet was complete, rooms were added to its inner face and a new tower built. Still later an external gatehouse was added and a chapel and tower created above battlement level. By 1572, however, it was abandoned.

◀Gate **A**, like that at **5D**, was protected by an internal barbican **B** butted up against the mantlet. It has a rebate for doors at one end **C** and a portcullis slot **D** at the other.

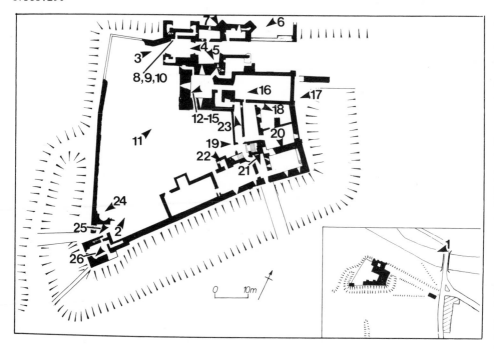

The field **A** to the south of the castle contains the rectangular earthwork remains of the Roman fort of *Brocavum,* located here, like the castle, to command the crossing of the Eamont **B**. Between the fall of the assumed Roman bridge and the present one built in 1811 there was only a ford, vestiges of which can be seen in hollow **C**.

2

E

B

C

D

A

▲
The general plan is that of a courtyard **A** with buildings around its sides. The keep **B** and gatehouses **C** form the principal block. Most buildings, like **D**, had pitched roofs **E**. The courtyard itself was levelled and made 'larger and handsomer' than it was before by Lady Anne Clifford in 1651. Forty years later Lord Tufton began demolition.

The curtain wall is not everywhere intact but at ▶ **A** its parapet survives and its breastwork can be traced **B**. There was no access from the curtain into the gatehouse as that building together with the keep formed an inner citadel.

3

B

A

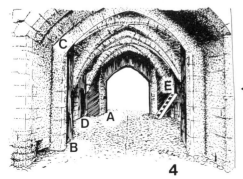

C

E

D   A

B

4

◀ Rebates **A** and **B** show that the inner gatehouse (probably late 13th century) had gates back and front. The latter was protected by a portcullis in slot **C**. The small room **D** was probably a guardroom while passage **E**, made defensible by having no permanent steps, led to a garderobe.

The outer gatehouse **A** built a little later than ▶
the other also had two gates and a portcullis.
Any attacker penetrating the outer gate passage would find himself halted by the inner
portcullis in this small courtyard and under
fire from the buildings around. The keep, for
example, was equipped with machiolation **B**.
The mortar line **C** is the remains of a relatively
modern lean-to but a much earlier roof crease
can be traced **D**. The building roofed by **D**
probably existed prior to construction of the
gateways for a structure built against wall **A**
would need only a single roof not a gabled one.

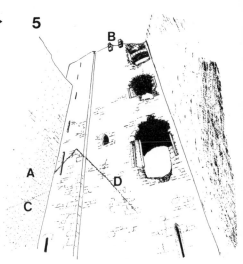

◀ The outer gatehouse carries an inscription **A**:
'Thys made Roger' — probably Roger Clifford
who died at Bannockburn in 1314. The plaque
has, however, been reset at the same time as
repairs were made beneath window **B** for in
both places the stonework is different from the
rest of the wall. The portal was defended not
only by its portcullis and gates but by machiolation **C**, and crossfire from wall **D** and
buttress **E**. This strength is, however, offset by
the four large windows, eg **B**. Their presence,
always assumed to be original, emphasises the
residential purpose of the top two storeys. The
absence of large windows from side **F** shows
the front of the gatehouse was meant to im-
press. The neat masonry face at **G** is evidence
that the ditch originally continued, as one
might expect, where causeway **H** now is. A
bridge would be needed and the otherwise
inexplicable masonry (of two different periods)
on **H** may be related.

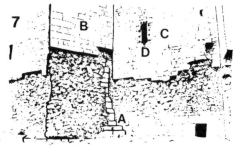

The squared stones **A** show buttress **B** once
stood unencumbered like **6E**, and that the
building connecting the two gatehouses **C** is
later. It was added to make communication
between the two easier. The holes for the iron
grill protecting window **D** are clearly visible. ▶

The buttress at the north west corner of the ▶
inner gate contained both a shoot **A** from a
garderobe and a postern with a 'Caernarvon
arch' **B**. The hole for the drawbar can be seen
inside at **C**.

8

9

▲
The postern was reached by an easily defended
spiral staircase from the portcullis room, the
only access to which was from the keep. Above
the portcullis slot **A** (**4C**) is a notched block
and two projecting stones **B** belonging to the
former winch. Window **C** was blocked when
the building between the two gatehouses **7C**
was added. The ceiling was of timber carried
on ledge **D**.

10

The fireplaces together with the large windows ▶
in the upper room show that this gatetower,
like the outer one, was designed to augment the
residential accommodation of the keep. The
upper room is probably that in which Lady
Anne Clifford died (1675).

The gatehouse **A** is later than the keep **B** for its ▶
stonework is different and it almost blocks
window **C**. The keep is typical of Norman ones
— square in plan with shallow clasping buttresses at the corners **D** and round headed
windows **E** lighting the upper floors — but
cannot be earlier than 1203 when the castle did
not exist. The building of the castle can be
dated to some time between 1203 and 1228.
The top of the keep **F** is, however, later still: its
masonry is slightly different, it has small
square headed windows and cruciform slits **G**.
When complete the corners were carried up as
turrets, eg **H**, and machiolation **I** was provided
in the centre of each side. This machiolation is
identical to that of the outer gatehouse suggesting it is the work of Roger Clifford.

The keep, excluding the turrets, was four
storeys high. The added top floor with its
corbelled corners **A** was octagonal in shape.
The springing stones and corbels of a basement
vault inserted in the 13th century remain at **B**.
At the same time a (now fragmentary) arcade **C**
was added to the walls of the principal apart-
ment. Flues at **D** show each main room except
the basement was equipped with a large fireplace. The surviving wall plaster belongs to
Lady Anne's restoration.
▼

11

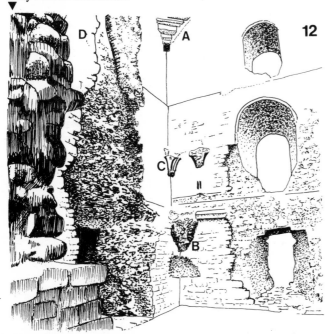

12

The passage from the stairs to the second floor ▶
room has a Roman tombstone **A** in its ceiling.
The formula of words is said to be Christian
and together with other tombstones, evidence
for a late Roman community existing around
the fort.

Corbels **A** carried beams for the floor of the
new top storey and the ceiling between those
beams was provided with a decorative coping
B. Prior to the addition of this new floor the
keep had a pitched roof, the gable of which can
be detected in line **C**. The roof was, however,
completely hidden by the surrounding walls, eg
D. **B** is probably the height of the original
parapet.
▼

The piscina **A** indicates this room was a chapel, the altar being beneath window **B**. Small room **C** with a cupboard in one wall was probably the vestry.

15

16

The original entrance to the keep was at first floor level through arch **A** which is more elaborate than any of the windows, eg **B**. The remains of its external staircase can be seen **C** cut through by a late 13th-century doorway **D**. Passage **E** would have been cut once the outer gatehouse had been added but door **F** is probably earlier. The staircase **C** was covered by a small building part of which survives in wall **G**. Bonding for the opposite wall can be traced at **H** and as holes **I** stop at this wall they must have housed joists for the roof. This forebuilding was demolished and a new one the full width of the keep — as shown by joist holes **J** and **K** — erected to provide a chapel or more probably great chamber. Doorway **L** was made to connect the new building to the keep's staircase.

17

▲
The south east corner of the great chamber, which is attributable to the 13th century, is represented by pilaster **A**. Wall **B** is butted up against it and built over the top so it was originally only two storeys high. The side of an external window survives at **C** and, like those in the outer gatehouse, appears to have been tall and, therefore, a military nonsense. The concentration of large windows around the entrance is noteworthy and their dating must be scrutinised particularly when they are compared with the small 14th-century windows **D** of the great hall. The wall of that building is not of one date, the plinths at **E** and **F** being different and there is a suspicion that the wall at **G** formed part of a structure earlier than **B** and that pilaster **H** was its corner.

18

▲
Above the timber floor which rested on corbels **A** was the great hall. It had a central stone hearth supported by masonry **B** and a doorway **C** connecting with the great chamber to which it was added in the late 13th century. In the 14th century new windows **D** and **E** (**17D**) were inserted and in the 15th century door **C** remodelled.

71

19

From the outside the hall was reached by staircase **A**. In the 14th century a corridor **B** was provided to link this with the keep (door **16F**).

The fireplace **A** shows the kitchen for the hall was at first floor level. Springers for the ribbed vault of the basement survive at **B**.

20

21

The barred window **A** and plinth **B** indicate the kitchen's west wall was once external. Wall **C** being of different character is later, as is the postern **D**.

22

The building added to the west of the kitchen **21C** was the chapel. Its large east window **A**, piscina **B** and sedilia **C** are easily recognised. Both ceilings and floor were of timber carried on corbels **D** and **E**.

Plinth **A** projecting into the 14th century corridor **B** (**19B**) marks the corner of the forebuilding covering the original entrance to the keep. The doorway into that building may have been in the same position as that of the later corridor **C** but is more likely to have existed at **D** where a vertical joint **E** can be traced. The butt joint **F** shows the forebuilding was heightened.

23

The semicircular foundation **A** is the only visible evidence for the bakehouse and brewhouse erected by Lady Anne on the site of earlier buildings. Here too would probably be stables. Note the postern **B**.

25

◀ This tower is contemporary with the inner gatehouse but unlike that tower has a door **A** opening onto the curtain wall **B**. The height of the breastwork is again visible, its inner face at **C** following the flight of stairs leading to door **A**. Presumably a tower existed at this corner prior to the present one and it may be that the early structure was the original gatehouse for which there is no other evidence. In favour of this is the causeway beyond the postern **24B**, the more elaborate earthworks at this angle than anywhere else (see plan) and the appearance of the present tower at a time when the old gate would have been abandoned for the new one adjacent to the keep. The other possible position is postern **21D** with a likely tower **17G**.

The fireplaces are indications of the residential ▶ character of parts of the tower.

26

The castle begun on the site of a Roman fort shortly after 1203 consisted of a stone keep within apparently timber and earthen defences. The keep was entered through a forebuilding but this was soon replaced by a spacious chamber. By the beginning of the next century the principal residential block had been transformed by the addition of two massive gate towers forming an inner citadel. Despite the great strength of this arrangement it is apparent that comfort was a major consideration both in the provision of light and in the amount of room available. The keep/gatehouse block would serve the lord and his family, buildings in the courtyard retainers and the south west tower followers of higher standing such as bailiff or constable.

The corbels **A** show that a building was constructed against the south side of the tower and there is evidence for it being of two periods. Blocked doorway **B** is, however, probably earlier than that building for it had a drawbar suggesting it was an external door reached by an external staircase. By the 17th century it had been replaced by a building with a steep roof **C**. Its eastern wall can still be traced **D**; its western side was at **E**. Doors **F** and **G**, which would thus be central, recall those often found between a kitchen and hall: the new building must have been a hall, the tower's basement the service end. This hall block was subsequently replaced by a building the whole width of the tower as shown by its corbels **A** being placed in the centre of the tower and by its shallow roof **H**. Its eastern wall was tied to the tower with stones in holes **I** and **J**. The lintel ▼

of doorway **K** which is a different shape to those of **F** and **G** probably belongs to this period as do the inserted sash windows **L** and battlements **M**. The windows provide an 18th century date.

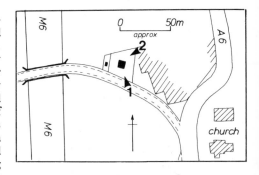

1

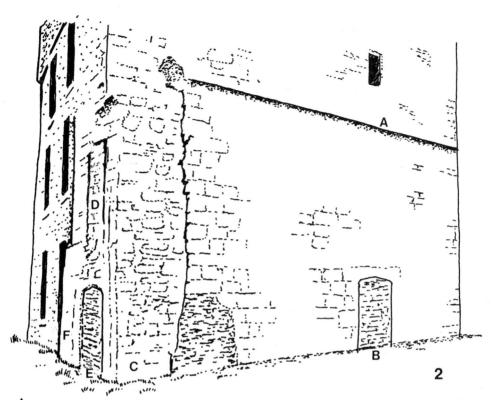

2

In that century a range was also added to the north side, its roof being at **A**. Its doorway into the tower **B** is in the same style as **1K**. At **C**, however, is the corner of a building earlier than the tower. This earlier structure must have remained in use when the tower was built for a first floor doorway was provided **D**. Its lintel was flat like that of **1B** with which it must be contemporary although door **E**, also in the corner of the old building, has a different head. The earlier wall **F** projects because the tower was not built at right angles to the old building. Why not, and why it should be joined on a corner, is difficult to explain.

The tower is not the earliest building on the site, it was added to a hall block exi.ting on a slightly different alignment to the north east. After construction of the tower a new hall was built to the south and this was replaced in the 18th century by a larger building. At the same time a new range was also added to the north and large windows inserted into the tower. All but the tower was demolished in the early 19th century. The date of the earliest buildings and the tower is not known but a 15th century date is likely.

21 EGREMONT CASTLE
NY010105

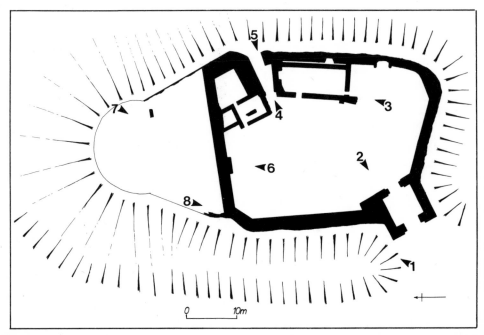

The plan of the present stone castle follows that of its timber predecessor. The bailey **A** was surrounded by a ditch **B** which also encompassed the motte **C**. This motte screened the bailey from the area to the north and was so dominant that the town there was named after it: Egre*mont*. Construction of the early castle can be placed between 1120 and 1138, between the granting of the barony and the siege by David I of Scotland. By the end of the century the timber curtain walls were replaced by stone ones in distinctive herringbone masonry **D**. Similar stonework in the gate tower shows it too was built by the end of the 12th century, although the masonry infilling its semicircular arch **E** and the present facing are probably 14th century. The curtain wall was also remodelled and a plinth **F** inserted into the earlier work to match plinth **G** of the gate tower. The tower had no portcullis to protect the gates, the raised drawbridge serving that purpose.

2

The entrance passage had a vaulted roof supported on corner columns, eg **A**. The rear portal was subsequently reduced in width by masonry **B**. A print of 1739 shows there were by then two storeys above, presumably entered from the curtain wall where a door can be traced **C**. This doorway shows the approximate height of the parapet walk.

3

Within the bailey were a number of buildings, originally of timber, backing on to the curtain. On the eastern side a long building was formed by wall **A** which originally continued at **B**. This range was sub-divided by wall **C** and the two rooms provided with fireplaces **D** and **E**.

Wall **F** is an addition for it blocks fireplace **E**. As room **G** would not have needed a new side wall if the curtain had been intact **F** must have been built when the castle was in decay. **G** is probably the courtroom which existed inside the 'ruinated' castle of 1578.

The chamfered stone at **A** is the corner of the ▶ long range once formed by wall **B** (3A). The creation of the postern **C** required this building to be truncated and a new end wall **D** erected. The fragmentary staircase **E** appears, however, to belong to the earlier building for where its fourth step should be there is only the rubble core of **D**. A fireplace, later reduced in width, existed at **F** with an oven (?) **G** to one side. Another possible oven **H** overlies a wall **I** belonging to the building constructed north of the postern after the demolition of the range represented by **A**. The splayed side of the postern **J** is a 'modern' repair the original shape being visible at **K**.

The curtain wall has been greatly patched both ▶ in antiquity and more recently. The masonry **A** which at first sight looks like a tower earlier than the curtain **B** is one such late repair, the original masonry being the flaking sandstone at **C**.

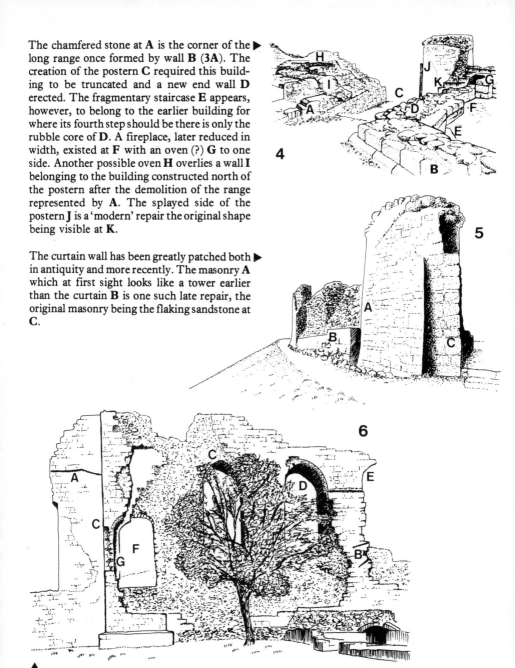

The existence of buildings on the western side of the bailey can be inferred by the roof line at **A**. Note the two periods of roofs to the east at **B**. While **C** is the southern wall of the principal residential block it is also revetting the motte upon which that building was placed. In its final form the main block was provided with at least three large windows **C**, **D** and **E**, suggesting that the great hall was located there. It was entered by door **F** which was defended by being raised above the bailey floor and by a portcullis in slot **G**.

7

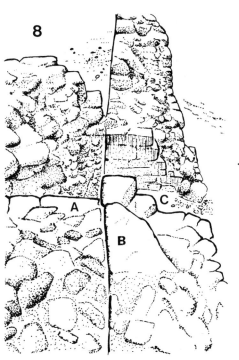

8

The building on the motte is shown in 1739 as being approximately square and with some form of internal division of which masonry **A** is all that remains. The defended entrance can leave little doubt that the building, which must have replaced at least one other, was intended to serve as a 'keep'. The earlier building(s) may have been circular but in the absence of excavation this cannot be determined. The face of the circular wall **B** overlies the foundation of the square 'keep' at **C** and so, in parts at least, is modern.

◄The southern wall of the 'keep' **A** has been butted up against the curtain **B** which must originally have continued around the lower part of the motte. Opening **C** was a garderobe pit.

> *The castle was built soon after the Norman conquest of Cumberland and consisted of a motte and bailey. It was soon rebuilt in stone and as a consequence its original plan became fossilised – a bailey with simple gate tower and citadel on the motte. By 1578 it was 'ruinated and decayed'.*

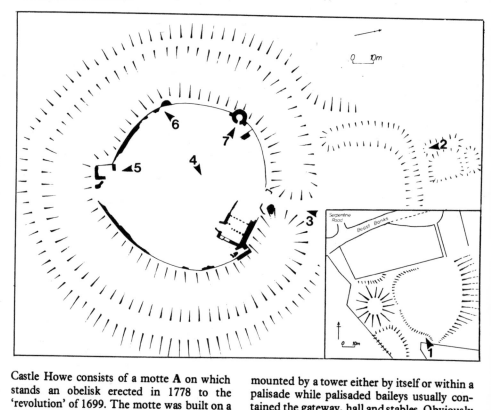

Castle Howe consists of a motte **A** on which stands an obelisk erected in 1778 to the 'revolution' of 1699. The motte was built on a natural ridge **B** from material excavated from circular ditch **C**. Only the top, therefore, is artificial. To the east is the much altered bailey **D** separated from the motte by ditch **C** which must have continued around the northern and southern sides **E** and **F**. The steep slope **G** required no ditch. Mottes elsewhere were sur-
mounted by a tower either by itself or within a palisade while palisaded baileys usually contained the gateway, hall and stables. Obviously the bailey had weaker defences and at this site the motte is placed on the weakest — uphill — side to protect it. Unfortunately the owner and, therefore, date of this castle is not known, but the first Norman baron of Kendal was Ivo de Talbois.

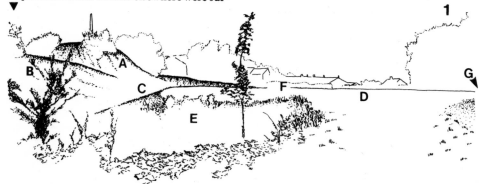

2

The castle to the east of the town has been built on a glacial mound. To the west it dominated the town, to the east was the castle park. The walled area **A** is circular in plan and is surrounded by a deep ditch with external bank **B**. North of the gateway **C** is a rectangular ditched earthwork **D** which was probably an outer court or garden. Beyond were fish ponds **E**.

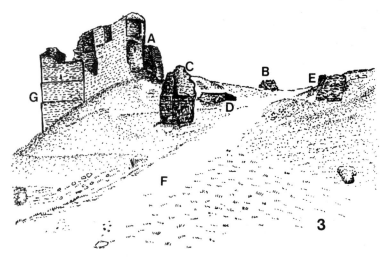

3

The main buildings of the castle were the hall block **A** adjoining the gatehouse at **B**. All that remains of the gatehouse is the detached masonry **C** and parts of the two flanking guard chambers **D** and **E**. Early drawings show the building had round fronted towers flanking the entrance. The causeway **F** is probably quite recent; the ditch was probably continuous and crossed by a drawbridge. The projecting towers of the gate and **G** would allow the defenders to rake the ditch and bank beneath the wall with fire without having to lean over the battlements. Tower **G** and the hall may be a 14th-century addition, the rest being surmised to be 13th century.

4

The hall, lit by at least three windows **A**, was at first floor level. Beneath were cellars **B** one containing a fireplace. Wall **C** suggests an extension to the south and there in tower **3G** the Lord and his family had their private rooms. This is shown by the sequence of rooms given in a survey of the partly ruined castle in 1572: 'no building left, saving only, on the north side is situate the front of the gatehouse, the hall with an ascent of the stairs to the same, with a buttery and pantry at the end thereof; one great chamber and two or three lesser chambers, and rooms of ease adjoining the same...under the hall are two or three small rows of cellars'.

5

6

Little survives of the large square tower at the south end of the castle although the remains of a vault **A** are identifiable. Much of the masonry has been repaired or added in the last two hundred years so the original character of the tower is difficult to determine. Its size suggests residential accommodation and its exterior projected beyond the curtain wall **B** and **C**.

Much of the present perimeter wall, eg **A**, is relatively modern, but fragments **B** and the outline **C** of the much thicker curtain wall survive in places. The solid bastion **D** with its splayed base must have been reached from the parapet walk of the curtain.

The vaulted basement of this tower was entered by door **A** and the room above has a fireplace opposite window **B**. There is no direct access between the two rooms so that the first floor level must have been entered from the curtain. The height of the first floor doorway from the ground, 14ft (4·2m), must be the approximate height of the parapet walk. Again, however, only fragments **C** and **D** of the curtain now survive. Projection **E**, containing a spiral staircase leading up from the first floor, appears in an 18th century drawing as a turret above the roof top. The garderobe visible on the exterior was also reached by the staircase. The thick wall **F** constructed against the curtain is part of a rectangular building of unknown purpose. It is shown, unlabelled, on a plan by Machell c1690. His record of a vanished chapel block and the mention of a 'dove cot' in 1572 shows there were once buildings in the courtyard.

Kendal possesses two castles, one of motte and bailey type the other a stone walled enclosure without a true keep. The construction date of neither is known but Castle Howe should be the earlier and it is generally assumed it was abandoned when the new stone structure was built. A possible occasion for this was c1184 when Gilbert Fitz Reinfred became baron through marriage to the heiress of the Lancasters (previous owners after the first baron Ivo de Talbois). As Gilbert and his wife were the first owners to spend much time in Kendal the 'new castle' is attributed to them. The first mention of a castle is, however, in 1215 when it was forfeit to the crown after King John captured Fitz Reinfred's son William in the siege of Rochester. Later restored to the family it eventually passed through the female side to the Parrs in the late 14th century. In 1543 Katherine Parr became the last wife of Henry VIII. Her brother died without heirs in 1571 and the castle, already in decay as the 1572 survey shows, was abandoned. It was acquired for the town in 1896 to mark Queen Victoria's diamond jubilee.

Visitors, who should call at the farmhouse first, will notice the frequent use of red sandstone for quoins, jambs etc, although the neat blocks at **A** are a modern repair, as is the walling of small stones **B**. This south eastern block **C** was two storeys high the lower one being lit by loops **D** with 14th-century heads, that above by much larger windows, eg **E**. The lower part of one such window **F** was blocked when the upper part **G** was remodelled in Tudor style. An early drawing shows **E** and **H** were similarly altered. Two curious details are the little window **I** with a finial above and the height of the inner side of the ditch **J**. West of **K** the ditch side is higher than to the east as if the front range **C** has been built at a lower level than the rest of the castle.

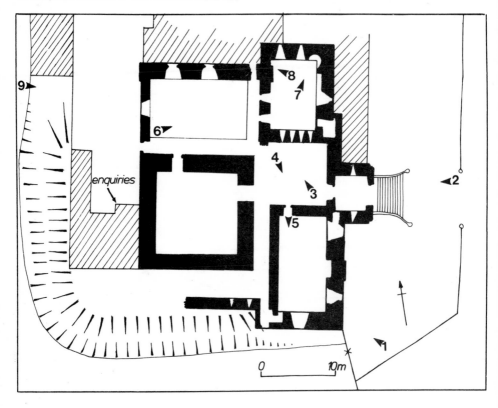

1

While the projecting gatehouse **A** is in the centre of the eastern side of the castle the loops in wall **B** have different heads from **1D** indicating the north east corner **B** is later than the south eastern one **1C**. The staircase **C** is certainly late belonging with the gateposts to the 17th century. There is no sign of steps earlier than **C** so the medieval means of entry ▼ must have been by drawbridge which, when raised, would have served as a portcullis protecting the outer gates. The arch of the inner gate **D** is 17th century although the jambs seem earlier and have holes for two drawbars on their inner sides. Examination of these will show one was withdrawn to the left the other to the right.

2

3

▲

The gate passage opened into a small courtyard whose western side was originally a wall at **A** through which was a gate with a portcullis slot **B**. Wall **A** must have been demolished when the great tower (present farmhouse) was built, and its continuation beyond **B** removed at an earlier time when **C**, the western side of the kitchen and eastern end of the hall, was erected. The south wall of the kitchen is even later for it is butted against the adjacent walls at **D** and **E**.

The character of the door **A** between the court-▶ yard and the south eastern block can be compared with that at **3B**. Here there was no strong portcullis but a single drawbar and decorative hood of 14th-century date. Such a weak entrance would need a protecting curtain wall so **B** with its gatehouse is probably contemporary. The room over the gatehouse, perhaps originally a chapel, was reached from the south eastern block or through **C** by a wooden staircase or ladder. At a later time it was furnished with a fireplace whose chimney **D** is 16th-17th century in date.

4

5

The south eastern block has been interpreted as a solar or great chamber. Lit by the large windows noted at 1 it had a wooden floor on joists **A** and a large fireplace **B**. The fireplace of the basement was directly below **B** but had no flue, only a smokehole — the curious window **1I**. The basement must also have contained a timber staircase leading to the room above.

6

The hall with its wooden roof supported by corbel **A** had two windows on its northern side. These are of 13th-century character and contain seats **B** and **C**. The dais for the lord and his guests must have been at the eastern end of the hall for there the window seats **C** are higher than at **B**. Normally the solar would be behind the dais but here there is a kitchen block with its characteristic screen **D**. The southern side of the hall has completely disappeared, perhaps it was demolished to make room for the great tower with its basement of two vaulted rooms entered through **E**, **F** being post 1872. The lost wall is, however, unlikely to have been south of corner **G** otherwise the gate with the portcullis **H** would have led directly into the hall.

89

7

The kitchen's fireplace **A** had a smokehole instead of a flue. At **B** are the remains of an oven.

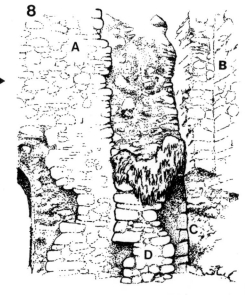

8

The kitchen walls **A** and **B** have been butted ▶ against the north wall of the hall hence vertical joint **C** and the short length of projecting masonry **D**. This is in agreement with the idea **2B** that the present kitchen block is later than the south eastern part of the castle and confirms that the eastern wall of the hall adjoining the portcullis gate **3B** has been rebuilt. What was here before the kitchen can only be determined by excavation but **C** must have been an external corner in the 13th century for it is faced with sandstone blocks, a characteristic of the corners elsewhere. Such a corner aligns through **3B** with the change in ground level noted at **1K** suggesting **D** was once the eastern side of the castle.

9

The north western corner of the hall remains intact **A** and protrudes beyond wall **B** showing the latter is not original. The lower part of **B** seems to be contemporary with the lower part of the great tower for the joint between them **C** does not extend to ground level. Their archway **D** had provision for a porch roof but no drawbar hole so it cannot have been an external door. The arrangement is reminiscent of Tudor garden gates suggesting the great tower might be of that date although some have linked it with a (odd) licence to crenellate in 1622. Whatever its date, wall **B** was not the external wall of the castle which must have been along the inner edge of the ditch **E**. The point at which the ditch and curtain turned to link up with the 13th century hall is not easily determined but if it were at **F** the hall would have projected. That it did so is suggested by the clear lines of corner **A** and it is interesting that **F** aligns with the portcullis **3B**. Was the hall a northern extension of an earlier castle?

In 1335 Sir John Huddleston was given a licence to crenellate and enclose with a dyke his dwelling at Millom. As the status of the Lords of Millom was only a little below that of baron his existing dwelling must have had some pretensions. The evidence suggests it was a moated manor house with a gate defended by a portcullis. The surviving hall may have been with or in addition to this area but the whole was altered after 1335 by the addition of the present eastern front and range, and presumably an extension of the moat. The north western corner of this extension was subsequently rebuilt and new kitchens provided. The great tower, which must represent an abandonment of accommodation in parts of the old castle, is probably 16th, perhaps 17th, century in date. When the buildings and curtain to the west of it disappeared is unknown but they must have been serviceable in 1644 when the castle was 'besieged' by parliamentary forces.

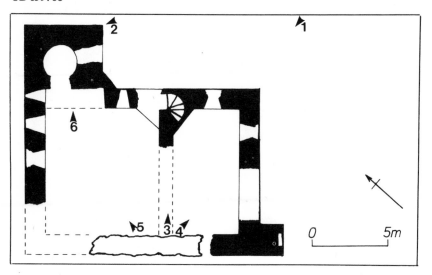

The tower is rectangular in plan with two projections **A** and **B**. **A** contains the garderobes, the sump for which survives at **C**. **B** could give covering fire to the entrance **D** inside which the drawbar hole is still visible **E**. Immediately inside the entrance was the main staircase lighted by small slits **F**. Apart from these the tower has two type of windows: large ones, eg **G**, and smaller ones **H** often possessing red sandstone surrounds. The latter, some of which are blocked, are the earlier of the two but are unlikely to be earlier than the 14th century.

2

▲
The battlements were carried forward on corbels **A** but this had no purpose other than to be decorative. That at **B** does however contain a rain water spout. The roof would be low angled and probably leaded.

3

◀The main rectangular part of the tower was divided by a crosswall **A**. Access to the upper floors was by the spiral staircase in the angle of wall **A** and the external wall. The first floor was reached through **B** but as this only opened into the north western half it was necessary to have a door through the crosswall to the south eastern half. One side of such a door can be traced at **C**. At second floor level the sequence is reversed, entry/exit being on the south eastern side **D**. Above this floor there were no other openings into the staircase although it ascended to roof level. The upper floors may have been reached by timber stairs within the rooms or by the privy stairs in wall **E**. Part of one such flight is visible at **F**. The base of the main staircase is tapered **G** but there is no evidence for this being a different period from that above. The taper seems simply to be the back of the treads, not hidden by a vertical wall because room **H** was only a basement.

As a basement, room **A** did not need a garderobe or fireplace like the other four floors above. The garderobes **B** were housed in the projection 1A. The use of sandstone for fireplace surrounds allowed some mouldings, eg **C**. In 1602, however, the tower caught fire. It was rebuilt and occupied again until unroofed and the timber sent to Knowsley (Lancs) in 1684-▼

90. The fire and rebuilding explains why there are both corbels, eg **D**, and joist holes, eg **E**, to carry beams for the wooden floors. Similarly the two periods of windows probably fall either side of 1602, the rebuilding being an opportunity to insert larger and more fashionable windows. The south western side **F** collapsed in 1884.

4

It is not known exactly when and for whom the tower was built but it was well appointed. On one side was a large kitchen and oven with three principal rooms above. Here too was a more private suite. On the other side was a series of poorer rooms although they too were heated. It seems unlikely anyone below a lord could afford such a place.

The north western half was four storeys high ▶
and not five as on the east. The greater height
of the rooms and the larger size of some fireplaces, eg **A**, show this was the residential side.
The separate stairs **B** and **C** suggest that the
rooms behind wall **D** and in (projection **1B**)
were a private suite. Below the principal rooms
was the kitchen with its fireplace **E**.

Behind the fireplace was a large domed oven **A**
which is so large it must have been heated by
first setting a fire inside and then raking it out.
The entry must have been via a door at **B**
showing one could walk down the side of the
fire. This helps explain the window **C**. The
three holes **D** must have helped support the
turnspit and other accoutrements.
▼

Monastic Remains

Monastic Work and Order

The different religious orders — Augustinian at Lanercost and Cartmel, Cistercian at Furness and Praemonstratensian at Shap — looked towards the same monastic tradition believing that the day should be devoted to three kinds of work: worship, meditation and writing, and labour on the land. The result of this common ideal was the similarity of plan between abbeys and priories of whatever Order:

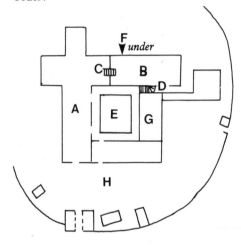

The church **A** was of primary importance and, therefore, the first building work undertaken was usually its eastern end. As some services were held at night time the dormitory **B** was immediately adjacent to the church, a staircase **C** linking the two. A staircase **D** for day time use led into the cloisters **E** which were for meditation and literary work. As maximum light was needed for this the cloisters were placed on the south side of the church. At Cartmel, however, the community had to resort to the unusual arrangement of cloisters north of the church. The other buildings around the cloisters were the chapter house **F**, refectory and warming house **G** and the western range with more accommodation for either individuals (at Shap and Lanercost the head of the house) or lay brethren (Furness). Beyond the cloisters was the outer court **H** with guest houses like those of Furness where the community could minister to travellers. Here too were gardens, orchards and farm buildings where the monks could work on the land.

Farming led to fields and tracks radiating from the monastery and required mills as at Shap. Sometimes, however the farm land was so far away that separate granges worked by a few of the community had to be established. Furness Abbey had numerous granges in the Lake District, eg Hawkeshead, and because they had the capital and organisation the monks were able to use better methods than their neighbours. Through grants they became major landowners, Furness having the powers and obligations of a lay magnate. The Dissolution of the monasteries thus had economic and social as well as religious consequences: innovative and capital intensive farming tended to cease, schools and travellers' accommodation disappeared.

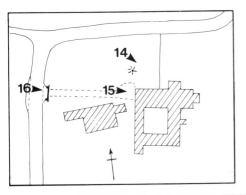

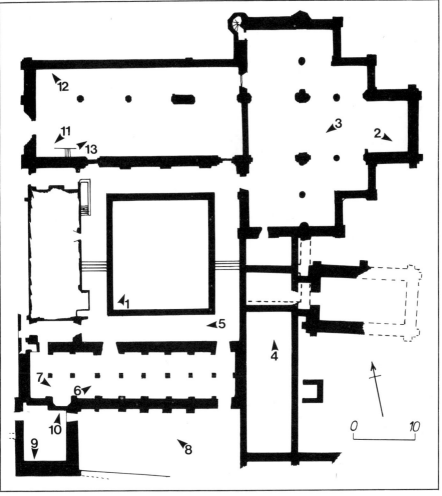

1

The buildings were grouped around the cloister court **A** and its alley **B**. The alley's roof was supported by corbels **C**. None are visible in the western range **D** because that was re-modelled after the Dissolution. Two doors **E** and **F** led from the cloisters into the nave of the church and a third **G** into the south transept. Alongside **G** was a holy water stoup **H**. **I** was a book cupboard, reading and writing being the principal activities in the cloisters.

The stonework of the nave above and below line **J** is different showing it was built at different times. As the upper part has simple early 13th century-lancet windows **K** the lower part must be late 12th century. This suggests that soon after being granted the site in 1166 the Augustinian canons built the eastern part of the church and the cloisters to the height of the alley roof **J** and then halted to gather more funds, completing the nave in the next century.

3

B ▲

3

▲

◀ The aisles of the presbytery stopped short of its eastern end so that a window on either side **A** could help light the high altar, behind which was the aumbry or cupboard **B**. The carved stonework **C** belonged to the piscina. As this was destroyed by coffin **D** the latter must be post Dissolution in date.

The church had the usual plan of nave (now beyond wall **A**), presbytery **B** and transepts **C**, **C** being the southern one. Above the crossing **D** was a central tower. The transepts and presbytery had aisles. That on the northern side was vaulted, the southern one had a timber roof on corbels **E**. Within the aisles were tombs of benefactors, **F** belonging to Sir Thomas Dacre.

4

5

On the south side of the cloister was the lavatorium **A** where the canons washed. The rough stonework **B** indicates the position of the stone troughs. Above the southern range at **C** was the refectory reached by a staircase at **D**. The present western range **E** has been greatly altered and much of the upper part belongs to the home built there by (another) Sir Thomas Dacre — fragments of ancient glass now in the present church carry the inscription 'In the year 1559 Sir Thomas Dacre, who was the first to come here after the Dissolution of the Priory founded this work...'. The monastic vault beneath the range was, however, retained and can be seen in **F**. An inscribed stone is built into the wall at **G**. It reads 'C. CASSI PRISCI' or Century of Cassius Priscus and was a building record or 'centurial stone' from Hadrian's Wall. The latter was used by the canons as a quarry.

◀ The walls of the building **A** on the eastern side of the cloister were tied into the south transept by the projecting stones **B** and **C** showing the eastern end of the church was built first. The roofline **D** indicates the eastern range **A** was two storeys in height, the upper one being the canons' dormitory. As the canons had to leave their beds for the night offices a staircase between church and dormitory was provided (door **E**). Below the night stairs was a small vestry entered through **F**. The projecting room **G** was the chapterhouse where the canons met each morning to confess their faults and discuss the business of the day.

It will be noticed that range **A** is narrower than the building indicated by roofline **D** and stones **C** and that a second roofline is visible **H**. **H** is the roof of building **A** and is later than **D** because its chapterhouse overlies the line of the walls which ran to **C**. As the first period walls **C** did not extend far the eastern range must have been modified at an early date. It is tempting to link this reconstruction with the Scottish raids in the early 14th century. In 1346 they burnt the cloisters.

The undercroft below the refectory was mainly for storage. The stones now kept here are of various dates, some medieval, some Roman. The roof was constructed of ribs **A** with panels of rougher work between **B**.

▼

6

▲
The chimney **A** is that of Sir Thomas Dacre's hall, the roofline **B** belonging to the earlier monastic building. The tower **C** is an addition for its neat corner **D** sits on top of an earlier wall **E** and at **F** it has been built against a buttress which unlike those at **G** and **H** has been preserved for most of its original height.

◀A wall partitioning this area from the rest of the undercroft must have existed, for the fireplace **A** indicates it was the warming house where at certain times of the day in winter the canons could come.

▲
The tower is, however, of two periods for wall **A** has replaced a thicker one **B**. The large windows and, therefore, wall **A** are unlikely to be earlier than Sir Thomas and probably most if not all of the fireplaces belong to him.

The lower part of the tower has already been▶ seen (**8F**) to be built against some monastic buildings and **A** here is the chimney of the warming house. Where the flue should be, however, there is the spiral staircase **B** which ends **C** at the height of the earlier, thicker wall (**9B**). **B** must be later than the use of the warming house ie post Dissolution but the earlier part of the tower could be monastic. There can, however, be little doubt that Sir Thomas used this as a pele tower.

11

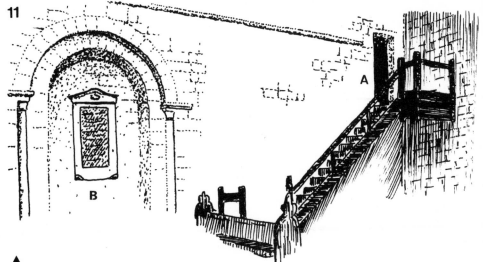

▲
At the western end of the church is a small, 15th- or 16th-century doorway **A**. The size suggests use by only one or two people at a time and if monastic was probably for a night stairs to a private suite of rooms either for guests or, more probably, the Prior. The blocked doorway **B** is one of the two which led from the cloisters into the nave.

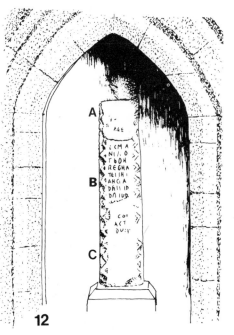

12

◀ Two inscriptions are carved on this cross shaft: **A** '. . . who was buried ye 20 July 1657 2nd yere of his age' and **B** (translated) 'In the 1214th year from the incarnation and the 7th year of the Interdict, Innocent III holding the Apostolic See, Otto being Emperor in Germany, Philip King of France, John King of England and William King of Scotland, this cross was made'. Evidently the cross was later used as a tombstone. Note the carved corner **C** of the shaft.

B

F

E

D

C

H

A

G

13

▲
The nave, which has only one aisle **A**, possesses a clerestory passage **B** which originally connected with that in the ruined eastern end (2). The blocking wall **C** was constructed c1740 to allow the nave to be used as the parish church. The nave was, however, built in two stages: the eastern end with its wide arch **D** and simple clerestory arches **E** identical to those in the presbytery and transepts, and the western end with the decoration of its clerestory **F** matching that of the lavatorium (**5A**). The eastern end of the church was, therefore, built first with a temporary wall at **G**, hence the short length of wall between arches at **H**. When the western end of the nave was added **G** was removed and probably replaced by a screen dividing the canons from the laymen who were allowed to use part of the nave for a parish church.

14

▲
A is the base of the inscribed shaft **12** for it has the same carved corners. Door **B** may have been the parishioners door into the church for after the Dissolution the parish church was housed in this aisle only later being extended to its present position.

15

16

The gateway into the priory precinct or outer
court must have consisted of a passage with
room or rooms above for the springers of a
vault **A** and **B** exist between walls **C** and **D**.
The slight earthwork running north **E** may be
the remains of the precinct wall.

◀ The western end of the church with its statue **A**
of St Mary Magdalene, Patron of the Priory, is
a fine example of 'Early English' architecture.
The passage or slype **B** provided access from
the cloister to the outer court (and vice versa).
In the outer court would be farm buildings and
guest houses of which tower **C** was part. In
1280, 1300 and 1306 Edward I stayed at the
priory; on the last occasion all winter.

*This Augustinian priory was founded in 1169
and shortly afterwards work commenced on the
eastern end of the church and south wall of the
nave/north wall of the cloister. The nave was
completed at the same time as the refectory. The
community was host to Edward I on a number of
occasions between and after which the Scots also
visited the canons – to burn and destroy. The
loss of income caused by the raids and the need to
pay for repairs after such events impoverished
the priory. After the Dissolution Sir Thomas
Dacre built his house in the western range and
utilised the guest houses. The parishioners were,
however, allowed to continue using part of the
church.*

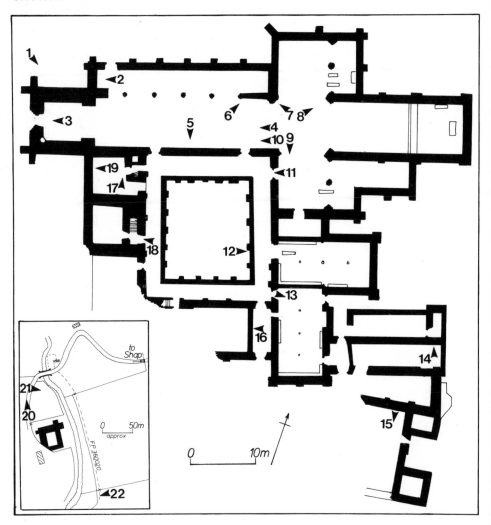

The tower stands at the western end of the ▶
church **A**. Niche **B** probably held a statue of
Mary Magdalene to whom the abbey was
dedicated. The brethren, Praemonstratensian
Canons, moved here c1201 from Preston
Patrick near Kendal. Why they moved is not
known but this is a more remote spot.

▲
The difference in stonework between **A** and **B**
is the result of the tower having been added to
the church.

3

The tower can be dated by the flat arched doorway **A** and other architectural details to the 15th century. Its building is generally attributed to Richard Redman who, while abbot, became Bishop of St Asaph in 1471, then Exeter in 1496 and Ely in 1501. Within 40 years of his death the abbey was closed — on 14 January 1540 it was surrendered to the crown.

4

The two roof lines **A** and **B** indicate the former ▶ height of the nave and that it had been reroofed after the tower was built. **A** must be the new roof as its apex is central to the tower while that of **B** is not. Doorway **C** beneath the window of the tower was the principal entrance of the church. Communication between the nave **D** with its single aisle **E** and the cloisters was by two other doorways **F** and **G**.

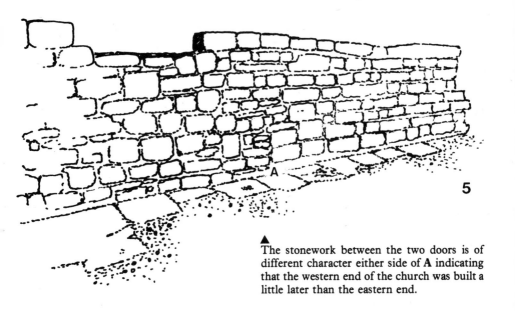

▲
The stonework between the two doors is of different character either side of **A** indicating that the western end of the church was built a little later than the eastern end.

5

6

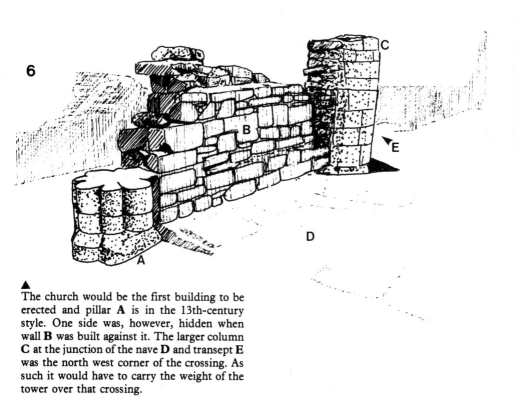

▲
The church would be the first building to be erected and pillar **A** is in the 13th-century style. One side was, however, hidden when wall **B** was built against it. The larger column **C** at the junction of the nave **D** and transept **E** was the north west corner of the crossing. As such it would have to carry the weight of the tower over that crossing.

The inserted wall **A** (**6B**) can be seen at **B** to have been built against another 13th-century column whose base **C** is visible below the present and late medieval surface. Much of the pillar has, however, been rebuilt in plainer style **D**. As this style does not continue at **B** it must be contemporary with or later than wall **A**. Similarly it does not extend to cover **C**

because it was built when the church floor was at its present level. The rebuilding of this north west corner of the crossing is attributable to structural failure of the old one caused by an attempt to raise the height of the central tower. Finding that impossible an entirely new tower, that at the west end, was built.

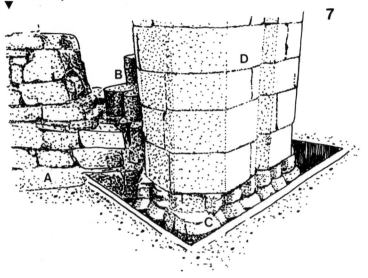

7

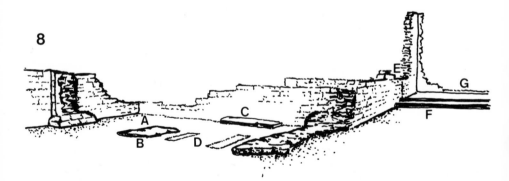

8

On the east side of the transept was an aisle **A** entered by two arches separated by pillar **B**. The two arches divided the aisle into two bays for use as chapels. In one, the base of an altar **C** and two grave covers **D** survive. The right-hand one has a crozier incised into its surface indicating the grave of an abbot. It was usual to

bury only abbots and benefactors in the church. A change in stonework at **E** indicates the presbytery was extended at some time, steps **F** being on the line of the original east end of the church. The remains of the high altar **G** can be seen inside the extension.

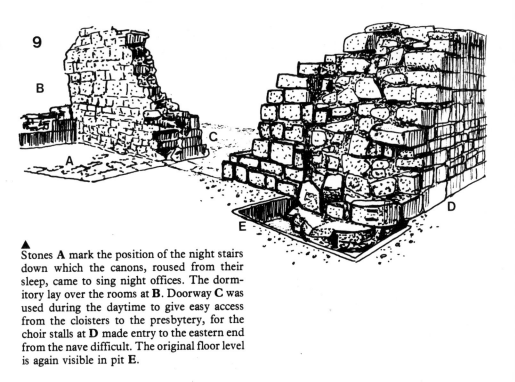

9

B

A

C

E

D

Stones **A** mark the position of the night stairs down which the canons, roused from their sleep, came to sing night offices. The dormitory lay over the rooms at **B**. Doorway **C** was used during the daytime to give easy access from the cloisters to the presbytery, for the choir stalls at **D** made entry to the eastern end from the nave difficult. The original floor level is again visible in pit **E**.

B

10

A

The circles incised into the later floor, eg at **A**, ▶ are thought to represent procession markers. On Sundays and special days a procession left the church's eastern end through **9C**, moved around the cloisters, and re-entered the church through **B** (**4F**). The procession then halted in two columns in front of the screen dividing the choir stalls from the rest of the nave. If this is the correct explanation then circle **A** must have been west of the screen ie the stalls were further east than **9D** when this new floor was laid. The stalls were probably moved when the presbytery was extended **8E**.

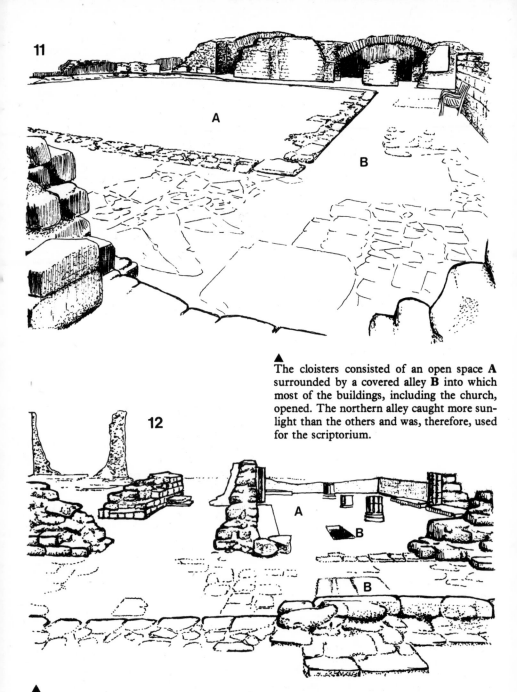

11

A

B

▲ The cloisters consisted of an open space **A** surrounded by a covered alley **B** into which most of the buildings, including the church, opened. The northern alley caught more sunlight than the others and was, therefore, used for the scriptorium.

12

A

B

B

▲ The chapter house **A** where the canons publicly confessed their faults and discussed the coming day's business was located on the eastern side of the cloister. The graves **B** like those inside the church would contain only important people. The ordinary canons were buried to the east of the buildings.

13

▲ The low bench **A** around the walls and large fireplace **B** indicate this room was the warming house. Here, at certain times of the day in winter the canons could have a fire. (The rest of the time they relied upon their numerous garments to keep warm). Like the chapter house the pillars supported a vaulted ceiling for the dormitory **9A** extended over both rooms.

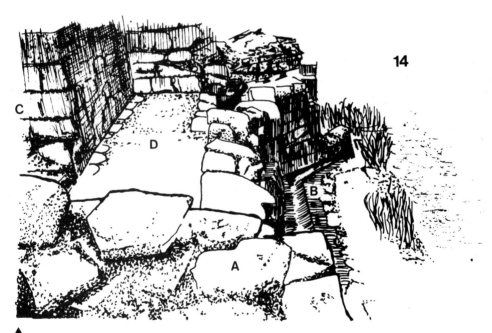

14

▲ Wall **A** was part of the dormitory's reredorter or lavatory, its drains **B** being flushed by the river. Room **C** built against the reredorter had its own garderobe **D**.

The springer of an arch **A** shows this building ▶ was two storeyed and it was almost certainly the infirmary. Its drains can also be seen in the river bank.

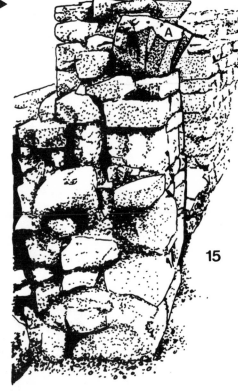

15

The infirmary was reached from the cloisters along a passage **A** in the southern range. The refectory would be located here at first floor level and the stairs in the thickness of the wall at **B** probably gave access. The original height of the walls is thought to be represented by corbel **C** in the farmhouse. Beneath the refectory was a vaulted undercroft of which only pillars **D** remain.

▼

16

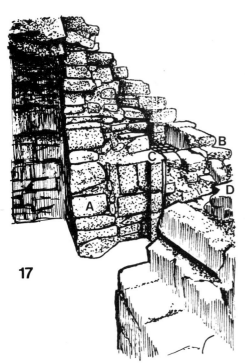

18

17

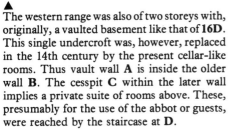

The western range was also of two storeys with, originally, a vaulted basement like that of **16D**. This single undercroft was, however, replaced in the 14th century by the present cellar-like rooms. Thus vault wall **A** is inside the older wall **B**. The cesspit **C** within the later wall implies a private suite of rooms above. These, presumably for the use of the abbot or guests, were reached by the staircase at **D**.

The provision of a staircase **A** so close to that of **17D** suggests the first floor was divided into two separate suites along the same line as the wall dividing the two cellars. Again the new vault wall **B** and its staircase is inside the original wall **C**.

Doorway **A** enabled goods to be brought into the undercroft from the outside. It was blocked when the new vault was built.

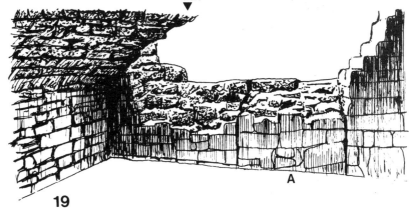

19

20

Beyond the main buildings are earthworks: two hollow-ways or tracks worn by vehicles and animals **A** and **B** and near their junction a corn drying kiln **C** indicate intensive farming around the abbey.

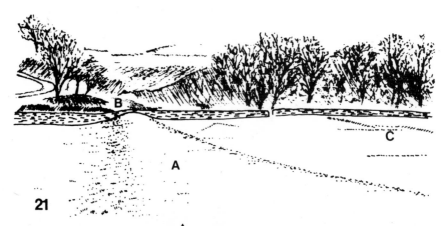

21

Embankment **A** which is too wide to be a buried wall must be the main road to the abbey. Its height above the river at **B** shows a bridge must have existed and as its western end is near the junction of the two holloways **20A** and **20B** it is probable the gate in the precinct wall was in the area of the present farm lane. Traces of other buildings and perhaps the precinct wall can be detected at **C**.

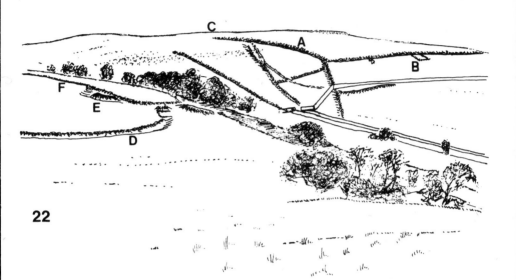

22

The field system of the abbey's home farm is visible as dykes or banks, eg **A**, on both sides of the river. At **B** are the remains of a barn which stood amongst those fields and it is interesting that the limit of the present fields **C** coincides with that of the medieval ones. The better quality land within that boundary compared with the moorland beyond is the result of continuous management since monastic times. Lane **D** led to the monastic mill **E** with its leat **F**. This carried water from higher up the river along the hillside at a gentler gradient than the river bed so that when it entered the mill it could fall onto the wheel. The lane shows the mill served a wide area. The canons, for example, had a grange or farm in the valley of Wet Sleddale to the south-east as well as numerous other holdings.

> The abbey was built by Praemonstratensians who had moved here from a less remote site. Their first building work was the construction of the eastern end of the church which they later extended. They also attempted to heighten the central tower with unfortunate consequences. Although located in a secluded valley on the edge of moorland the abbey became the centre of well tended enclosures which supported corn. Despite this and land holdings elsewhere, the abbey was not vastly rich when it was surrendered in 1540.

27 HAWKESHEAD HALL
SD349988

The only ancient part of the hall remaining is the gatehouse with a niche **A** over the passageway. As such a niche can be paralleled in a number of monastic establishments, eg Cartmel **9A**, and remembering that Furness Abbey held the manor of Hawkeshead the building was probably their grange or farm. **A** therefore contained a statue of St Mary, Patron of the Abbey. The room at first floor level is sometimes referred to as the court room (for manor courts) and it is possible it served the same purpose in medieval times, being the local administrative centre for the abbey's estates and interests, which were vast.

▼

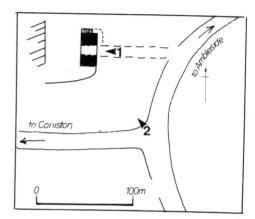

A   2

▲
Certainly the site is well suited to be such a centre being near a meeting of routes. In medieval times there was probabiy no bridge over the stream, only a ford. What may be a lane leading to a ford can be seen at **A**. The courtroom suggests the grange was ranged around a courtyard at **B** but window **C** being in the gable and original — possibly 13th century — shows the gatehouse either projected beyond that courtyard, or had no building on its south side. An old farmhouse did, however, occupy the southern side of the presumed courtyard until the early part of the last century. With its destruction many clues about the surviving building must have been lost.

The site in the early nineteenth century

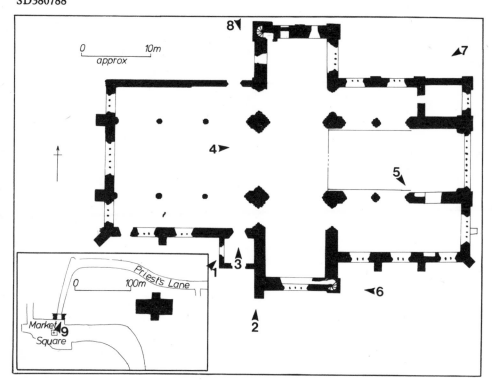

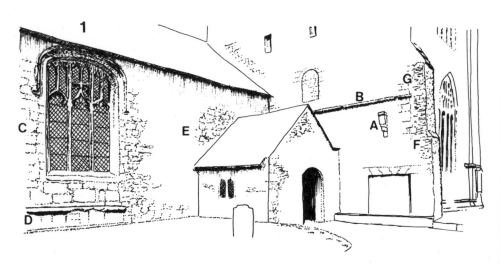

F

C

D

E

G

B

A

2

The church is the usual cruciform plan with a central tower above the crossing. The tower was heightened in the 15th century by the addition of the unusual diagonal storey. A cloister was laid out on this (the south) side of the church the roof of its alley, carried on corbels **A**, meeting the transept wall below course **B**. There is, however, no such provision in wall **C** implying the latter was built when the cloisters no longer existed. **C** must, however, have been constructed upon lines contemporary with the cloister for it contains two doorways, the usual arrangement between cloisters and nave. The wall is certainly of two periods: **C** with its limestone blocks and plinth **D**, and **E** of irregular limestone and no plinth. The earlier wall of the transept is of freestone. Buttress **F** is again different and was built to tidy up the jagged end **G** of the transept. This line shows the lower part of the transept wall continued or was to be continued along the
◀ eastern side of the cloister.

▲
Above the eastern range **A** would be the canons' dormitory. To allow night time communication between there and the church a staircase was provided through (blocked) doorway **B**. Its semicircular arch like that of blocked window **C** dates the transept to the late 12th-early 13th centuries. The early work in freestone with a projecting course **D** is continued at **E** showing the present aisle of the nave **F** is on the line of the early one. The porch **G** was built in 1626.

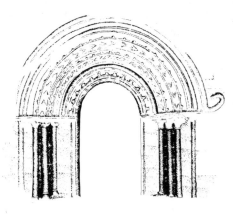

◀ This elaborately decorated doorway is part of the early aisle wall and is characteristic of the 12th-early 13th centuries.

As at **2E** the freestone walling of the eastern end of the church turns into the nave and stops **A**. The implication is the transepts **B** and **C**, presbytery **D** and crossing **E** were built first. Their construction can be dated to the early 13th century by the 'Early English' arches, eg **F**. The intention must have been to continue the nave in the same style for a pillar **G** was provided to receive a nave arch. The latter, however, are simpler in style indicating a dislocation in the building programme. The halt to building had occurred by 1229 when the Abbot of York granted indulgencies to those supporting the fabric of the church and three years later the Pope himself had to take it under his protection. The nave was completed in two stages, the eastern bay first (wall **1E**), the rest of the nave in the 14th century (wall **1C**).

▼

The early part of the church contained a tri-▶
forium **A** but this was never continued into the
nave as planned. The presbytery **B** was separated from the aisle on either side by two semicircular arches **C**. Originally the presbytery
projected beyond the aisles so that a window on
either side, eg **D**, could help light the altar. **D**
was blocked in the 14th century when the
southern aisle was lengthened, probably at the
expense of Sir John Harrington who lies with
his wife in the tomb at **E**. His role as a major
benefactor must explain his tomb being allowed to cut the sedilia **F**.

That the aisle was widened as well as lengthened is shown by its wall **A** blocking the original
lancet window **B**. The plinth of the new wall **C**
is the old one taken up and re-used.
▼

7

▲
The slight break **A** in the line and quality of the projecting course shows where the aisle's roof originally ended and its pitch is visible in line **B**. The two blocked windows **C** and **D** indicate the eastern wall of the presbytery was originally lit by an arrangement of lancets until the insertion of the present great window **E**. The precise date of **E** is not known but it is in Perpendicular style and may therefore be contemporary with the raising of the central tower in the 15th century. An alternative interpretation is that it forms part of the restoration of 1617, the presbytery having been unroofed for the previous eighty years.

The north transept is like the southern one ▶ except that it has no round headed windows (**2C**) only lancets **A** and **B**. That at **B** was, however blocked and a doorway **C** inserted for night stairs when the dormitory and cloister were moved here. The corbels for the alley roof of the cloister can be seen at **D** and **E**.

This major and unusual change has been attributed to destruction of the old cloisters by the Scots in 1316 and 1322 but this is unlikely for two reasons. Firstly, the Lanercost Chronicle records the Scots left the priory alone and, secondly, at Lanercost where the cloister was destroyed it was rebuilt on its old site.

A much earlier date for the change is implied by the semi-circular arch of **C** and the absence of any blocked windows in the north wall of the nave. This evidence is consistent with the cloisters having been moved in the early 13th century before the nave was complete and the

8

reason for their removal probably the same as that which caused the intervention of the Pope **4**.

The problem may have been with the original grant. The priory was founded c1190 by William Mareschal who brought a number of Augustinian canons here from Braderstoke in Wiltshire. As, however, there was a parish church already in Cartmel an accommodation had to be worked out between the canons and the locals. In this context it is interesting that within ten years of William's death, with the

▲ The 14th-century gatehouse to the monastic precinct had a statue of the Virgin Mary, Patron of the Priory, in its niche **A**. The passageway **B** was closed with gates which opened inwards, and the room above would be for a porter. Guest houses would also be somewhere in the vicinity. The juxtaposition of the gatehouse and town square demonstrates the economic role that monasteries played.

eastern end complete, work stopped and high authorities were called in. Could it be that William's successor refused to back the project and the locals successfully demonstrated a right to the area taken for cloisters?

That the eastern end made provision for a grander nave with a north aisle wider than the present one is shown by roof line **F** projecting further than, and course **G** stopping short of, the present aisle.

The Augustinian canons began building almost immediately after 1190 and by 1220 had completed the eastern end of the church with provision for a matching nave. A major problem then arose, however, and the nave was completed to a smaller and simpler design. Perhaps related to this the cloisters had to be moved to the north side of the church. In the 14th-century part of the nave – probably that used by parishioners – was rebuilt and completed and in the 15th century further alterations were made. The church was saved from total destruction at the time of the Dissolution by being a parish church.

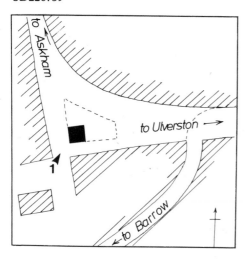

This building was a principal administrative centre for Furness Abbey for here the abbot kept secular court and housed prisoners. In its present form it has been greatly altered: the windows and doors suggest a 14th century date while stonework **A** and the internal arrangements are 19th century. The corbels **B** indicate a building stood at **C**, its roof presumably joining the tower beneath the projecting course **D**. There is no evidence for the walls of the building being bonded into those of the tower so they must have been constructed later or been of timber.

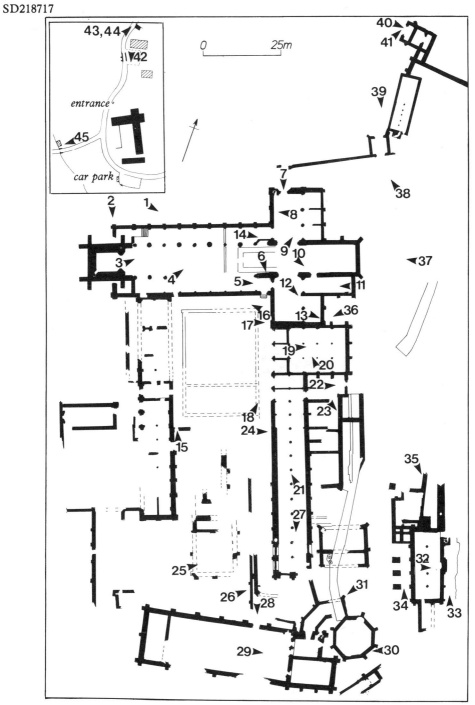

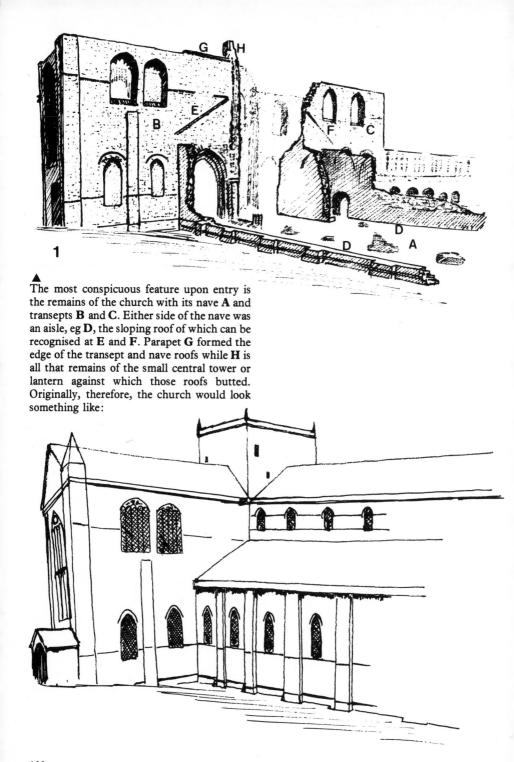

1

▲
The most conspicuous feature upon entry is the remains of the church with its nave **A** and transepts **B** and **C**. Either side of the nave was an aisle, eg **D**, the sloping roof of which can be recognised at **E** and **F**. Parapet **G** formed the edge of the transept and nave roofs while **H** is all that remains of the small central tower or lantern against which those roofs butted. Originally, therefore, the church would look something like:

2

The great belfry tower at the western end of the church was adorned with statues in niches such as **A**. That part of the church had to be demolished to make way for the tower is shown by the aisle walls **B** overlapping those of the tower. It seems that when the monks wished to build the new belfry they found there was insufficient room between the western end of the church and the valley side as it then was. As the construction of the tower destroyed the original western entrance to the church another was provided in the new wall built at **C**. The doorway and stairs **D** are those by which the lay brothers entered the church from their dormitory at night.

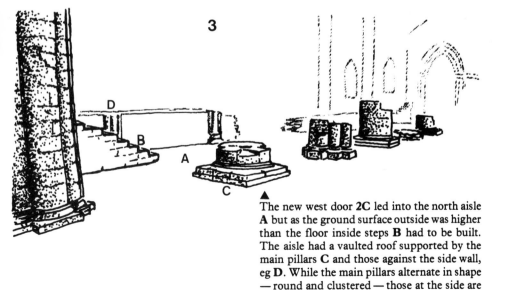

3

The new west door **2C** led into the north aisle **A** but as the ground surface outside was higher than the floor inside steps **B** had to be built. The aisle had a vaulted roof supported by the main pillars **C** and those against the side wall, eg **D**. While the main pillars alternate in shape — round and clustered — those at the side are all in the clustered design.

4

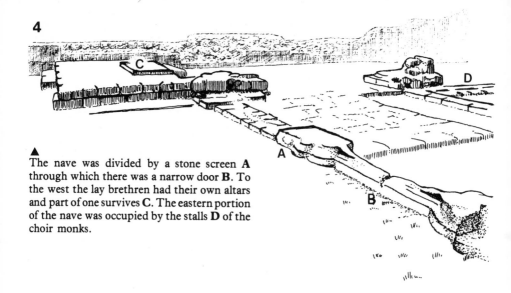

▲
The nave was divided by a stone screen **A** through which there was a narrow door **B**. To the west the lay brethren had their own altars and part of one survives **C**. The eastern portion of the nave was occupied by the stalls **D** of the choir monks.

5

As the choir monks spent much of their time in ▶ either the cloisters or their stalls it was usual to have a doorway between the two **A**. This door opened into the south aisle where the wall pillars **B** are of an earlier design than the clustered ones of the northern aisle **3D** indicating wall **C** is earlier than most of the present church. Arch **D** shows the shape of the aisle's vaulting, the rough stonework **E** being the filling between the intersecting ribs. The flat upper surface of the filling formed the floor of the triforium — the triangular space between the vault and the sloping roof **F**. At **G** are the remains of one of the arches between the nave and the triforium. Door **H** originally gave access but had to be blocked when the walls suffered structural failure, causing the arch of **H** to distort. To help prop the crumbling wall the arch between the aisle and transept **I** was also blocked, only a small doorway **J** being left.

The first arch or bay of the nave **A** has also been blocked up presumably for the same reason: the south western pillar of the crossing **B** was weak if not collapsing. It was one of only four — one at each corner of the crossing —

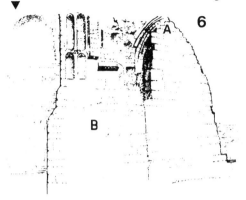

▼

which supported the central tower and it may be that an attempt to heighten that part overloaded the old masonry. Even without adding more weight the masonry must have been suspect for the monks, unable to find solid rock, had built on platforms of great oak logs. The result was that some walls such as those of the chapterhouse and north transept tipped slightly outwards. The low lying ground also caused other problems and the original floor was soon raised to its present level — the original is 13in (30cm) below.

The door into the north transept may have been the principal entrance into the church. The reason for this unusual arrangement was the cramped position of the site (as seen at **2B**). The style and decoration of the door is late 12th century.

Excavations have shown joint **A** to be the north west corner of a transept earlier than the present one. On the evidence of door **7** which belongs to the new or extended transept the building was enlarged in the late 12th century.

▼

9

10

▲
The arches **A** opened into the triforium above the aisle **B** of the enlarged transept. In each of the three bays of the aisle was a small chapel and altar, eg **C** and **D**. Part of the rich floor remains at **E**.

◀ The main or high altar **A** stood at the eastern end of the presbytery, with the elaborately carved sedilia **B**, piscina **C** and aumbry **D** on the south side. The great east window **E** and large windows on the northern side were in the perpendicular style of the 15th century. It would have been structurally difficult to insert such large windows into an earlier presbytery so this part of the church with its timber roof on corbels **F** must have been rebuilt at that time. The earlier presbytery which would also have had a timber roof can be dated by the round-headed arch, eg **G**, on either side to the later 12th century. The arches which had opened into the side chapels of the transepts, eg **9C**, were walled up to support the central crossing when the presbytery was remodelled. The 15th century doorway **H** was provided for access to the sacristy where the vestments were kept.

The sacristy was created in the 15th century ▶ from a bay **A** in the south transept's aisle. The bay's exterior wall was demolished except for the lowest courses **B** retained as a step, and an extension built at **C** by the construction of wall **D**. The timber roof and its corbels **E** replaced the stone vault **F** of the old bay. The partly demolished arch **G** is more intact on the other side of the wall **10G** showing wall **H** has been modified more on this side than at **10**. Within the new facing of **H**, however, a shadow of the old bay's wall **B** can be seen at **I**. This was caused by **B** having been left standing while **H** was altered on either side. When work on **H** was complete the old wall was demolished and the scar in the face of **H** patched.

Wall **A** (**11D**) partitioned the sacristy from the other two bays **B** and **C**. As the wall is vertical while pillar **D** leans the structural damage noted at **6A** and elsewhere had occurred or was stabilised by the time the sacristy was built in the 15th century. The staircase **E** was the night stairs used to link the church and choir monks' dormitory and would originally have continued into the transept. The projecting stone **F** was probably designed to hold a light and it has been suggested the corbels **G** supported a clock.
▼

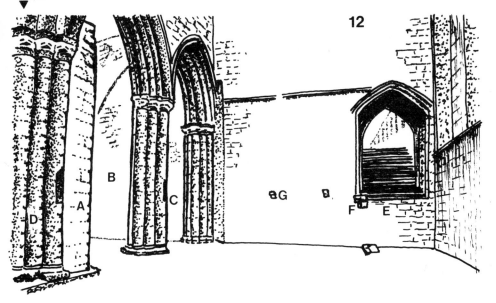

After the construction of the sacristy the▶ remaining bays of the transept **12B** and **12C** retained their original use as chapels as indicated by this magnificent piscina. The drain hole in the basin is clearly visible.

13

The exact purpose of this wall built between existing pillars is not known but it was not a simple buttress like **6A**. As a main entrance to the church was through the north transept this wall was probably a screen — with a loft reached by staircase **A** — separating the choir monks from the area where laymen might come. It is known that in the 14th century pilgrims started coming to the church to see a statue of the Virgin Mary and it was probably then that the monks felt the need to insert a screen for privacy.
▼

14

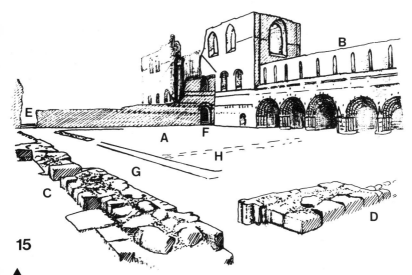

15

The main buildings were arranged around the cloister court **A**. At first floor level on the east **B**, west **C** and south **D** sides respectively were the monks' dormitory, the lay brethren's dormitory and the refectory. The church occupied the northern side, its nave having two doors **E** and **F** into the covered alley **G** which went round all four sides of the cloister:

On Sundays and special days a procession left the church by door **F** proceeded round the cloister and re-entered the church at **E**. Excavations have shown the present rectangular cloister was preceded by a square court with a refectory occupying its south side. The south side of this small cloister is marked out at **H**.

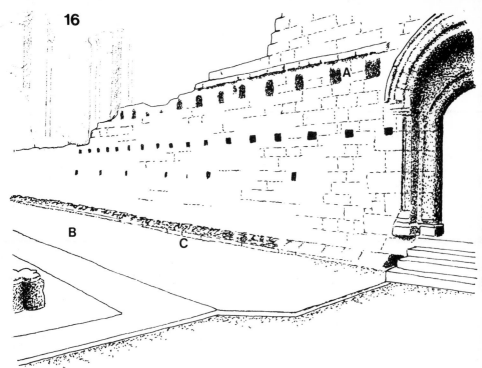

▲

Holes **A** were for the timbers forming the roof of the cloister alley **B**. The bench **C** is a reminder that this northern alley was the one which got most sunlight and was, therefore, where the scriptorium was located. The only book known to have been written here and to have survived is the *Chartulary* or *Coucher Book*. It contains a portrait of the author working in the scriptorium:

The *Chartulary* is in two volumes each of which begins with a metrical account of the abbey:

'In eleven hundred and twenty four
Was Furness first founded and sited.
Its first founding was doubtless at Tulket, and
second at Bekansgill, where now
It is founded. Three years and three days had
Elapsed...
In Tulket were we grey monks, but here
We are white, as we know by this dress
In this vale Count Stephen did build this house
The peer whom the people of England after
Entitled their king...'

From this it will be learned that the abbey was first founded at Tulketh near Preston in 1124 (probably 1123) by Stephen then Count of Boulogne later King of England. In 1127 the monks moved to the present location because it was more isolated. The valley was at that time known as Bekansgill and for a while the abbey was known as St Mary's of Bekansgill. Until 1147 the monks belonged to the small Order of Savigny which used grey habits but in that year the Order became Cistercian with white habits. The abbey was closed in 1539 when there was an abbot, prior and 28 monks.

The absence of projecting course **A** from the ▶
wall of the eastern range **B** is evidence that the
latter was built after the church. This is con-
firmed at **C** where the stones of the eastern
range are carefully tied into those of the transept, part of which can be dated to the 12th
century by the round-headed doorway **D**. This
has been shown by excavation to belong to a
church earlier than the present one:

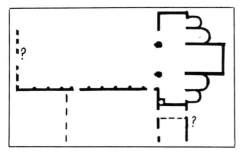

The earlier transepts were a different shape
and, as has been seen at **8**, they were shorter.
Door **D** led into a passage or slype between the
south transept and what was intended to be the
eastern range. Part of an arch can be traced at **E**
suggesting a little work on the eastern range
had been carried out when the new transept
was extended over it. To this first work also

belonged the square cloister and early refectory
15H. As the extended transepts date (**7**) to the
late 12th century it is probable the alterations
were made when the monks became Cistercian.

18

▲
The round headed, deeply carved arches and
lancet windows above date the present eastern
range to the late 12th-early 13th century. Arch
A led into the chapter house while recesses **B**

and **C** were probably bookstores — books
being the principal feature of cloister work. **D**
would be the parlour where the monks could
talk if necessary and **E** was the new slype.

19

▲
It would be in the chapterhouse that the decisions to send monks out to start daughter houses were taken. From here monks established Calder (W Cumbria), Rushen (Isle of Man), Swineshead (Lincs) and, indirectly, Byland (Yorks). In addition they founded another two houses in Ireland and were given control of another and its two dependencies. The windows are in the plate tracery style of the 13th century and the vaulted ceiling remained intact until the 18th century. Above was the dormitory with its timber roof on corbels.

20

When the south transept **A** was built provision ▶ was made for an eastern range or dormitory lower in height than that actually erected. This is inferred from roof line **B-C** ending below the tops of the dormitory windows **D**. The large window **E** is late, the original arrangement being two round headed windows **F** and **G**.

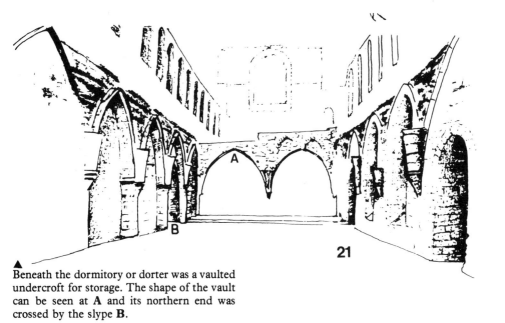

▲
Beneath the dormitory or dorter was a vaulted
undercroft for storage. The shape of the vault
can be seen at **A** and its northern end was
crossed by the slype **B**.

▲
Wall **A** built against the buttress of the chapter
house **B** is thought to have been erected after
the abbey was dissolved. Contemporary writ-
ings indicate the presence of a house and farm
buildings at that time.

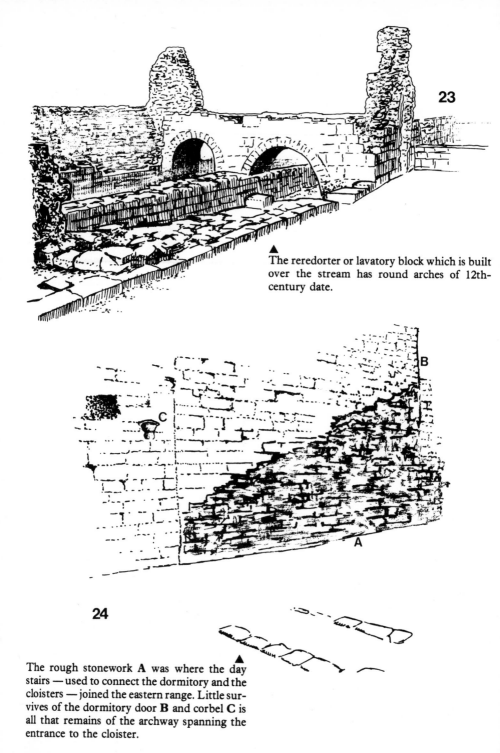

23

▲ The reredorter or lavatory block which is built over the stream has round arches of 12th-century date.

B

C

A

24

▲ The rough stonework **A** was where the day stairs — used to connect the dormitory and the cloisters — joined the eastern range. Little survives of the dormitory door **B** and corbel **C** is all that remains of the archway spanning the entrance to the cloister.

25

▲

When the first refectory was pulled down **15H** and the cloister enlarged the new dining room was built north-south, not east-west as the original had been. One corner of the new building survives **A**. The warming house was at **B**.

26

▲

The southern end of the eastern range consisted of a number of open arches **A**, **B** and **C** which were later walled up. The reason for these arches is not known but they emphasise the undercroft **21** must have been for storage. At **D** is one side of a doorway which in the absence of a corresponding side appears together with its wall **E** to have been part of an unfinished building. The latter does not make much sense if the eastern range had already reached its present extent so **D-E** must be regarded as earlier, and in this position may have been intended as an infirmary.

143

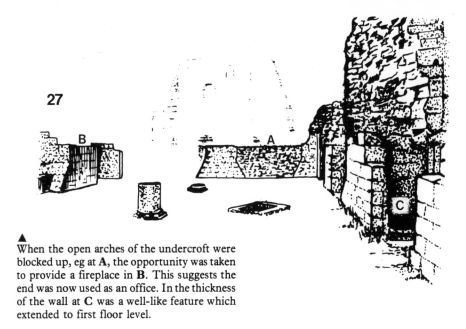

27

▲
When the open arches of the undercroft were blocked up, eg at **A**, the opportunity was taken to provide a fireplace in **B**. This suggests the end was now used as an office. In the thickness of the wall at **C** was a well-like feature which extended to first floor level.

28

▲
On the skyline to the south is the precinct wall **A**, inside which are a number of old field boundaries or dykes, eg **B**. The wall seems to cut this field system and may, therefore, be identified with that built by Abbot Bankes in

1516. In 1516-17 William Caase and his wife took Abbot Bankes and his monks to court. The Abbot was indicted of having 'pulled down the whole town called Sellergarth... wherein there were 52 tenements and tenants ... and ... laid the third part of the said town to several pasture to his own use'. (Lancs and Cheshire Record Soc, Vol 32, 1896).

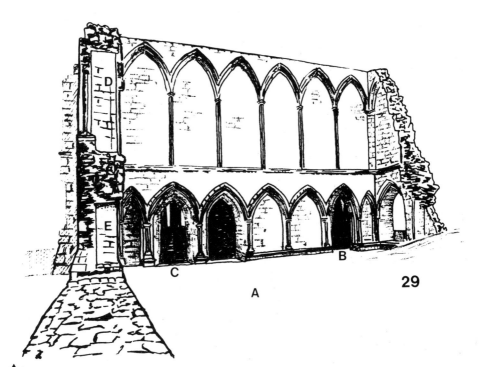

The infirmary consisted of a large hall or ward **A**, chapel **B** and buttery **C**. It is not certain whether the hall had two floors but it did possess windows at two levels **D** and **E**.

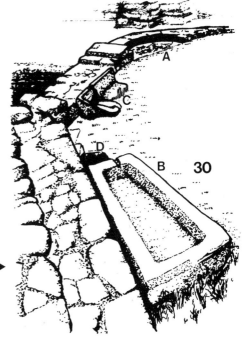

The infirmary was served by this octagonal ▶ kitchen with its fireplace at **A**. The remains of two troughs **B** and **C** and a refuse chute **D** also survive. A drain hole can be seen in **B** and there are records of lead piping having been found near the building.

31

▲
The kitchen was approached from the infirmary by a passage **A**. Its eastern end is visible at **B** so it must have been built across the stream with the kitchen door at **C**. The height of the passageway can be gauged by the walls at **D** and it may have carried an upper room at the infirmary end — door **E** does not make sense otherwise. The spiral staircase **F** presumably finished in a turret. The triangular windows of the chapel **G** place the infirmary no earlier than the 14th century.

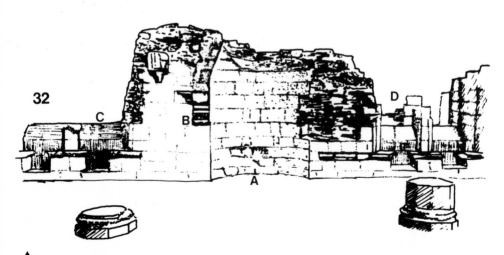

32

▲
This building, interpreted as the earlier infirmary, possessed a fireplace **A** with a stone hood or canopy supported by corbels **B**. On either side were windows **C** and **D** containing seats, fragments of which remain.

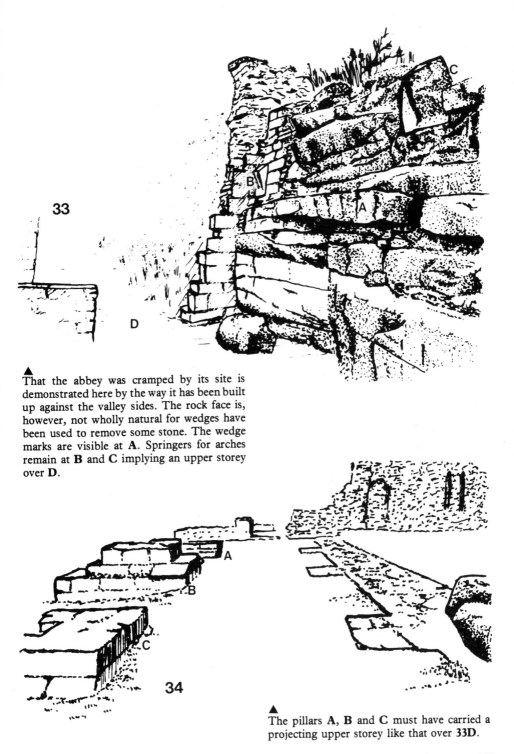

33

That the abbey was cramped by its site is demonstrated here by the way it has been built up against the valley sides. The rock face is, however, not wholly natural for wedges have been used to remove some stone. The wedge marks are visible at **A**. Springers for arches remain at **B** and **C** implying an upper storey over **D**.

34

The pillars **A**, **B** and **C** must have carried a projecting upper storey like that over **33D**.

35

The projecting storey was supported here by a massive wall **A** through which passage **B** provided light for window **C**; an odd arrangement which can only be explained if **C** and the infirmary it lit were already in existence. As the triangular arch **B** shows this extension took place at the same time as the building of the new infirmary **31G** the addition of an upper storey here is interpreted as being a conversion of the old infirmary into lodgings for the abbot. In its hall with its splendid fireplace he could entertain important guests. Before this he must have lived at the south end of the dorter block, an arrangement not unknown elsewhere. Interestingly, the southern end of the dorter in this abbey was served by a well **27C** similar to that included in the extension here **D**.

The aisle of the south transept had two roofs: a ▶ timber one on corbels **A** and a vaulted one with triforium between it and the roof proper **B**. The timber one is the later for its roof **C** cuts across the blocked door **D** of the triforium. The decorated stones **E** are, however, a mystery for they would have been hidden whichever roof was in use and they are not neatly coursed, as if they were simply later infill. They may or may not be linked with the carved stones **F** and **G** in the wall above. That wall can be dated by the blocked window **H** no later than the middle of 13th century. Stones **F** and **G** must have come

36

from the unfinished first church and it is tempting to see their inclusion here as evidence for the abandonment of a (planned) highly decorated church when the monks changed to the 'puritan' Cistercian order.

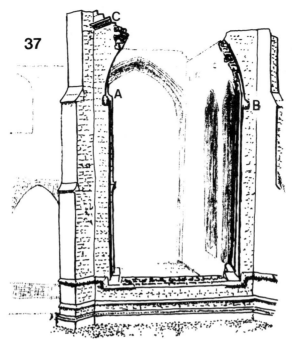

37

The large east window of the church had a
hood ending in two stone heads: a king **A** and a
queen **B**. Tradition says these represent
Stephen and his queen. The moulded course **C**
indicates the rebuilt presbytery was provided
with a fashionable low pitched roof.

The monk's cemetery was surrounded by a
wall **A** with a small gatehouse **B**.

38

149

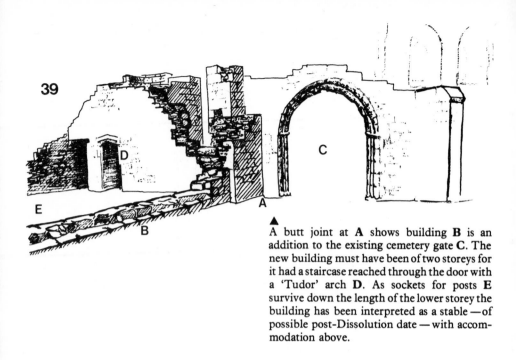

39

▲ A butt joint at **A** shows building **B** is an addition to the existing cemetery gate **C**. The new building must have been of two storeys for it had a staircase reached through the door with a 'Tudor' arch **D**. As sockets for posts **E** survive down the length of the lower storey the building has been interpreted as a stable — of possible post-Dissolution date — with accommodation above.

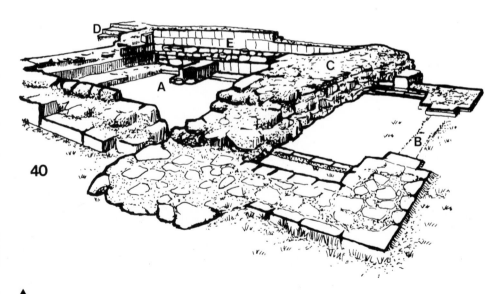

40

▲ A building with two doorways **A** and **B** in 12th-century style has been overlain by another **C** which had an upper floor reached by a staircase at **D**. The new wall was built in places with rubble foundations **E** directly on top of the earlier wall. The early structure must, therefore, have been buried to the level of **E** before the new floor was laid and its walls have been incapable of being utilised. This could only be if it was totally ruined or had never been built above one or two courses high.

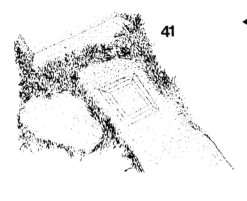

41

Scratched on the threshold of door **40A** is the layout for the game called 'nine men's morris' or 'merrells'. It has been suggested that this was done by school boys. Their existence is known since local people testified in the reign of Elizabeth I to the generosity of the monks: 'the tenants did receive weekly ... 60 barrels of single beer or ale ... that the tenants of Newbarns and Hawcoat had all the dung ... weekly 30 dozen of coarse wheatbread, and sufficient iron for their ploughs ... timber for repairing their houses ... two persons to come to dinner one day in every week ... and that it was lawful for the tenants to send their children to school ... and such children were allowed to come into the hall every day, either to dinner or supper'.

In this statement can be seen both the wealth and generosity of the monks and around the abbey there must have been brew houses, a bakehouse and extensive stables. Apart from the needs of the lay brethren the latter were kept for guests.

42

Little remains of the main guest house except the entrance passage **A** between rooms **B** and **C**. Alterations, whereby pillars were enclosed in a later wall, can be seen at **D**.

43

▲
Outside the gatehouse was a chapel **A** with a
statue in the niche **B**. The gate and wall **C** were
moved here in the 18th century.

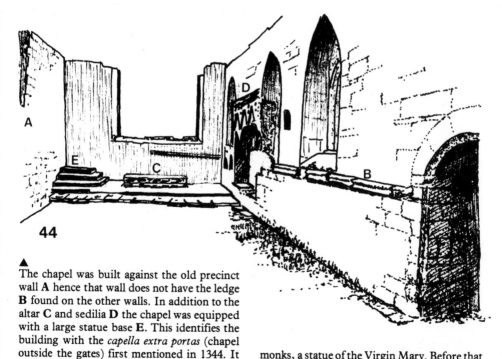

44

▲
The chapel was built against the old precinct
wall **A** hence that wall does not have the ledge
B found on the other walls. In addition to the
altar **C** and sedilia **D** the chapel was equipped
with a large statue base **E**. This identifies the
building with the *capella extra portas* (chapel
outside the gates) first mentioned in 1344. It
was erected (against the precinct wall) for pilgrims to venerate, without disturbing the
monks, a statue of the Virgin Mary. Before that
date they seem to have been allowed into the
north transept **14**.

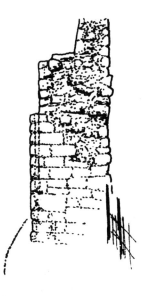

45

▲
The western gate in the precinct wall is smaller than usual and had only one room over the passageway, presumably for the porter.

The abbey's location in a narrow, secluded valley caused problems of layout. The main approach and entrance could not be from the west as was usual, instead the main gatehouse was to the north with a principal entry into the church being in the north transept. When established in 1123-4 the monks belonged to the order of Savigny but soon they adopted the Cistercian rule. During the Savigny period work started on the eastern part of the church and the layout of the cloister. This scheme was, however, soon modified, the transepts being enlarged and the cloisters extended by the demolition of the refectory. The abbey had achieved most of its present form by the middle of the 13th century. Some time after the church had suffered structural problems the presbytery was rebuilt in the latest fashion and a great tower added at the western end of the church. By the 16th century the abbey was very wealthy, the second richest Cistercian house in England. While the monks were often generous to their tenants they could also turn them out of their homes. The monks themselves were dispossessed in 1537, soon after which the church was allowed to be a quarry. Some buildings were, however, kept in use and new ones added to form a gentleman's house and farm. See also Dalton and Hawkeshead.

Glossary

Apse Semicircular end of a building or space.

Aumbry Cupboard or recess in the wall for sacramental vessels.

Bailey Courtyard surrounded by a defensive perimeter.

Barbican Projection (normally in front of) a gateway, the idea being to allow defenders on its walls to fire at the back of the enemy trying to break down the main gate.

Bay Structural division of a roof, normally the area between pillars.

Bronze Age This loose and somewhat outdated term is applied to that period between approximately 2,000 BC and 800 BC.

Butt Joint A wall derives much of its strength from having the vertical joints overlapping. When two lengths of wall have been butted against each other because they were built at different times a single vertical joint often results:

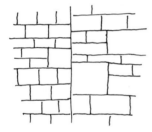

Cist Box-like arrangement of stones, usually for burial.

Choir monks Those whose principal duties were literary and worship. The manual jobs were often undertaken by largely illiterate members; the lay-brethren.

Clerestory The row of windows above the aisle roof which lit the central area directly.

Conventual Belonging to the convent — in its original sense the community, whether male or female.

Curtain Wall The perimeter wall between two towers.

Decorated style 14th century. The windows were often filled with ornamental tracery or divisions.

Draw bar Doors were often secured by a horizontal baulk of timber, usually removed by sliding into a hole in the adjacent wall.

Finial Pinnacle, often over a canopy.

Freestone Rock which is easily carved, usually a sandstone.

Garderobe Latrine often at the end of a passage or recess in the wall.

Jamb Side post of a doorway.

Lancet Early 13th-century style of window, narrow with a pointed head.

Lay brethren See choir monks.

Machiolation Construction of the battlements well forward of the rest of the wall allowing the defender behind to drop missiles through the parapet floor:

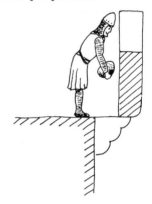

Motte Large conical mound.

Mullion Vertical bar in a window.

Nave Western part of the church.

Neolithic New Stone Age, approximately 4200-2000 BC.

Perpendicular Style 15th century, wholly English. Lighter walls, larger windows with flatter arches. To keep the glass in place the window space was divided by vertical and horizontal members.

Pilaster Square column like a shallow buttress.

Pivot stone The stone in which the bar in the bottom of a door turned — a hinge.

Piscina Small basin with a drain beside an altar for washing sacramental vessels.

Plate tracery 13th century. Two lancets covered by a hood or moulding with holes through the space between the hood and windows.

Plinth Projection of a wall near ground level.

Quoin Corner stone.

*pivot
stone*

Reredorter   Building containing latrines.
Revett   Face, support, retain.
Ridge and furrow   Numerous low ridges just a few yards (metres) wide caused by a method of ploughing no longer practised.
Scriptorium   Area where books were written or copied.
Sedilia   Seats for officiating priests.
Slype   Passage.
Solar   Upper room, lord's private area.
Transepts   The arms of a cross shaped church.
Triforium   Gallery between the main arches and the clerestory.

Index

abbeys, see monastic
Abbot Bankes, 144
Aldingham, 48
Ambleside, 34, 35-8, 40
Anglo Saxon Chronicle, 52
Appleby Castle, 48
apse, 154
Arnside Tower, 48, 92-5
artillery, 51, 53, 56
Askham, 22
astronomical alignments, 9, 10, 14, 20
Aughertree Fell, 8, 22, 23ff
Augustinian, 98, 126
Aumbry, 98, 134, 154
auxilliary, 34
Avalon, Isle of, 47

bailey, general, 154
bakehouse, brewhouse, 53, 60, 74, 151
Bannockburn, 66
barbican, 48, 52ff, 61f, 154
Barrow Museum, 20
bay, 154
Beaker, 19
Beetham Hall, 48f
Bekansgill (Abbey), 138
Bewcastle, 26
Black Death, 7, 33
book cupboard, 98, 139
Borrowdale, 29
Bradestoke, 126
Brigantes, 7
Bronze Age, 7, 9f, 12, 14-26 passim, 154
Brougham, 12, 48, 64-75
Burgh-by-Sands, 26
burial mounds, 7, 9, 15-18 passim, 23, 26
Burwens, 6, 8, 22, 27f
Byland Abbey, 140

Caase, Wm, 144
Calder Abbey, 140
Caldew, river, 57
Caldewgate, 57
Camden, 15
Carlisle Castle, 48, 50-7
    museum, 42
    siege of, 48
Carrock Fell, 22, 25f
carvings, prehistoric, 9f
Castle Howe, Kendal, 82, 85

Castlerigg, 13f
castle gateways, 48
castles, general, 48, 75, 84f
    timber, 48, 52, 79, 82
Cartmel Priory, 96, 120, 122-7
chapter house, 96, 101, 114, 133, 139f, 141
Chartulary, Furness, 138
Chesters, 46
church screen, 105, 113, 132f
cist, 16, 18, 154
Cistercian, 138, 148, 153
clerestory, 105, 154
Clifford(s), 12
    Lady Anne, 65, 67f, 74
    Roger, 66, 68
Clifton, 48, 76f
cloisters, 96, 98, 110, 114, 116, 123, 126,
    132, 137ff, 142
cohort, 34, 44
collared urn, 17, 20
Collingwood, 47
conventual, 154
Copeland/Ravenglass, 7, 47
Coucher Book, Furness, 138
court, Medieval, 120, 128
Cromwell, 56
Crosby Ravensworth, 8f, 16ff
curtain wall, 154

Dacre, Sir Thomas, 99f, 102f, 107
Dalton, 6, 22, 32f
Dalton in Furness, 128
decorated style, 154
deer park, 27, 83
Denton, 26
deserted village, 33, 144
Dissolution, 96, 98ff, 103, 106f, 119, 127,
    138, 141, 150, 153
drawbar, 60, 67, 76, 87f, 92, 154
drawbridge, 52f, 60, 79, 83, 87
droveways, see outgang
Dunmail, king, 7
    Raise, 7

Eamont, river, 9, 64
Eden, river, 51, 57
Egremont, barony of, 47
    castle, 48, 78-81
Esk, river, 40

field clearance cairns, 28
fields, 21, 24f, 28, 31, 33, 96, 119, 144
finial, 154
fish ponds, 53, 83
funeral feasts, 17
Furness Abbey, 96, 120, 128, 129-153

garderobe, general, 154
Gaythorne, 9
German Engineers, 51
Goggleby stone, 15f
granges, 53, 96, 119f
great chamber, 70f, 89
great hall, 60, 71f, 80, 82ff, 89
Great Mell Fell, 14
Greenwell, Canon, 17

Hadrian, 34, 38, 45
Hadrian's Wall, 51, 100
Hardknott, 34, 39-45
Harrington, Sir John, 125
Hawcoat, 151
Hawkeshead, 96, 120f
Helm, 29
henges, 9, 12, 14
hillforts, 7, 25f, 29
Hollin Stump, 16
Huddleston, Sir John, 91
hypocaust, 43f, 46f

inbye land, 25
infirmary, 116, 143, 145-8 passim
Ireland, 140

jamb, 154

Karl Lofts, see Shap
keep, castle, 48, 52, 54-7 passim, 65-70
    passim, 72f, 75, 81
Kendal, 48, 82-5
kerbed mounds, 9, 17f
Keswick, 9
kiln, corn, 19, 118
    meat, 63
King Arthur's Round Table, 8, 9, see also
    Mayburgh
King Arthur, 12, 13
    David (Scot), 57, 79
    Edward I, 54, 107
    Edward II (charter), 57
    Eveling, 47
    Henry I, 52
    Henry VIII, 50, 56, 85
    John, 85, 104
    Philip (France), 104
    Richard III, 63
    Stephen, 57, 138, 149
    William II, 52
    William (Scotland), 104
kitchen screen, 76, 89
Knowsley, 94

Lady of Fountain, 47
lancet, 154
Lanercost Priory, 96, 97-107, 126
Lanercost Chronicle, 48, 126
lavatorium, 100, 105
leper hospital, 47
Levens, 8f, 18f, 22
Long Meg, 8, 9ff
Lyons Garde, 47
Lyvennet, 7, 28

Mabon, 47
Machell, 85
machiolation, 59, 66, 68, 154
Malory, 47
manor house, 47f, 91
manorial hall, 76f, 91, 94f
Mareschal, Wm, 126
Mayburgh and Round Table, 9, 11ff, 14
Medieval land use, 27, 33, 96, 118
megalith, erection of, 16
Merrels, 151
Millom, 48, 86-91
mills, 96, 119
moat, 48f, 91
monastic, benefactors, 99, 112, 114
    cemetery, 114, 149
    church, first buildings, 98, 105, 111, 119,
        124, 132f, 139
    dormitory, 101, 113, 115, 123, 126, 131,
        135, 137, 140ff
    economic impact, 7, 96, 120, 127, 151,
        153
    guests and guest houses, 96, 104, 106f,
        117, 148, 151
    orders, 96
    precinct wall, 107, 118, 127, 144, 152f
    refectory, 100, 116, 137, 143
    ritual, 113, 137
    road, 118
    choir, 132, 135, 137, 154
monks, lay, 96, 131f, 137, 154
Morgan, 47
motte, general, 154
motte and bailey, 48, 78ff, 82, 85
Mullion, 154

Muncaster, 47

nave, 154
Neolithic, 7, 9, 10, 13-17 *passim*, 19, 21
Newbarns, 151
Ninemen's Morris, 151
Norham, 59
Norman Conquest, 7, 52, 81

orthostats, 28, 31
outgangs, 22, 25
ovens, 80, 90, 95
palace (medieval), 54
Parr, Katherine, 85
pavement circles, 20
pele, 49, 76f, 88, 91f, 103, 128
Pendragon Castle, 13
Penhurrock, 18
Penningtons, 47
Penrith Castle, 48, 58-63
perpendicular style, 154
Piercebridge, 21
pilaster, 154
pilgrimage, 136, 152
piscina, 70, 73, 99, 134, 136, 154
pivots, 34, 37, 41, 154
plate tracery, 154
plinth, 154
plough, Romano British, 21-2
Pope, the, 104, 124
population charges, 7f
portcullis, 53f, 60, 65ff, 79f, 87-91 *passim*
post Roman, 21, 47
Praemonstratensian, 109, 149
prehistoric ritual, 20, *see also* funeral feasts
  timber buildings, 9
premedieval, 24, 33
Preston Patrick, 109
Principia, see Roman HQ
protection of sites, 8

quarrying (Medieval), 51, 59, 100, 147
quoin, 154

Ravenglass, 40, 45ff
Redman, Richard, 110
Reinfred, Gilbert Fitz, 85
reredorter, 155
revett, general, 155
Rheged, 7, 28, 47
ridge and furrow, 14, 155
ringbank, 18f
ring cairns, 9, 17f
ringwork and bailey, 48

Roman, 7, 21, 26, 28ff, 34, 51, 57
  advance into Scotland, 45
  bath house, 34, 44ff
  bridge, 64
  centurial stone, 100
  civil settlement, 36, 69
  inscription, 42
  military desposition, 34
  parade ground, 39
  road, 36, 45
  stones, 51, 101
  tombstone, 69
Roman forts, Ambleside, 7
  Brougham, 64
  Carlisle, 57
  Hardknott, 39
  arrangement, 34, 38, 40
  barracks, 34, 37
  CO's house, 34, 37, 43
  defences, 34f, 40
  development, 34, 38, 40
  granaries, 34, 38, 43f
  HQ, 34, 38, 42
  strongroom, 38
  workshops, 34, 37
Rothay, river, 35
rural de-population, 33
Rushen, abbey, 140

St Cuthbert, 6, 85
Savigny, 138, 153
'scale', 26
schools, Medieval, 96, 151
scriptorium, 138, 155
Scottish raids, 7, 48, 57, 59, 79, 101, 126
Sealford, 6, 22, 30f, 33
sedilia, 73, 125, 134, 152, 155
Sellergarth, 144
settlement, 7, 21
  native, 21f
  Scandinavian, 22, 47
Shap Abbey, 96, 108-119
Shap Avenue, 8, 15f
sieges, 48, 79, 85, 91
siege engines, 57
shielings, 22, 26, *see also* transhumance
Skara Brae, 21
Skellaw Hill, 15f
slype, 155
solar, 84, 89, 155
stone circles, general, 7, 9, 17f
  purpose of, 9, 11
  maths, 14
Stonehenge, 12

158

Strathclyde, Kingdom of, 7
Strickland, Wm, 59
Sunbrick, 9, 20
sunken lanes, 23, 118
survival of evidence, 8, 27, 31
Swineshead, abbey, 140

Talbois, Ivo de, 82
Trajan, 34
transepts, 155
transhumance, 8, 26
triforium, 125, 132, 134, 148, 155
Tufton, Lord, 65
Tulket, 138
'tun', 22, 23

unenclosed huts, 7, 19

vicus, *see* Roman civil settlement

Walls Castle, 8, 46f
wall plate, 27
warming house, 96, 102, 103, 115, 143
Wet Sleddale, 119
Whitehall, 48f
Windermere, lake, 35

York, Abbot of, 124
Yugoslavia, 34